Advanced Reviews for *The Simple Care of a Hopeful Heart*

Posttraumatic growth flows when we do not romanticize or play down our pain, but open up to new possibilities not available had the pain not occurred in the first place. In *The Simple Care of a Hopeful Heart,* Dr. Robert Wicks, a world-renowned expert and author on resiliency and self-care, shares the importance of knowing how to mentor ourselves, so we do not simply seek to bounce back from psychological pressures and darkness, but actually harness them to achieve deeper self-understanding. This book is a much needed guide for these challenging times.

Bradley T. Erford, PhD
Professor, Peabody College of Education and Human Development
Vanderbilt University
Former President, American Counseling Association

Through stories and anecdotes, as well as his wisdom as a long-tenured psychologist and author on the themes of self-care and maintaining a healthy perspective, Dr. Wicks takes the reader on a journey to explore how to use challenges and pitfalls wisely as vehicles to become stronger and more resilient. Especially now, with the world we once knew upended with COVID-19 and societal discord, this book is the proverbial shot in the arm we all need to bolster our "immunity" in order to actually thrive when facing adversity.

Linda Laskowski-Jones, RN
Fellow, American Academy of Nursing
Editor in Chief
Nursing2020 Journal

The Simple Care of a Hopeful Heart is a treasure trove of insights and wisdom to help us navigate through a climate wrought with anxiety, fear, and uncertainty. With his signature charm, vulnerability, wit, and unique perspective of life's challenges, Dr. Wicks inspires readers to transform hardships into opportunities, roadblocks into possibilities, and resentment into compassion. His lessons shine a much-needed light of hope and promise not only in the present darkness of a pandemic but through the storms of life that happen in all eras.

Therese Borchard
Author, *Beyond Blue*
Associate Editor, Psych Central

Praise for Previous Related Trade Books by Robert J. Wicks

***The Tao of Ordinariness: Humility and Simplicity in a Narcissistic Age* (Oxford University Press: 2019)**

Selected as a 2019 Best Book of the Year by *Spirituality and Practice*

". . . with wit and wisdom garnered from literature, philosophy, and psychology, this book is a great guide for everyone seeking to explore the possibilities within themselves."

Stephen Joseph, PhD
Author, *Authentic: How to Be Yourself and Why It Matters*

* * *

***Night Call: Embracing Compassion and Hope in a Troubled World* (Oxford University Press: 2018)**

"Robert Wicks, a renowned psychologist and specialist in the area of resilience, has written a truly impressive book."

Robert Brooks, PhD
Faculty, Harvard Medical School;
Co-author of *The Power of Resilience*

* * *

***Perspective: The Calm Within the Storm* (Oxford University Press: 2014)**

"This is the kind of book you can't put down because it is so necessary."

Alexandra Fuller
The New York Times best-selling author of *Cocktail Hour Under the Tree of Forgetfulness*

* * *

***Bounce: Living the Resilient Life* (Oxford University Press: 2010)**

"Insightful, practical, and often humorous, *Bounce* is the right tonic for the spirit we need in a stressful world."

Helen Prejean
Author, *Dead Man Walking*

* * *

Riding the Dragon
(Sorin Books: 2003/2012)

"Like a good friend's support in tough times, *Riding the Dragon* is compassionate and wise."

Jack Kornfield
Author, *A Path with Heart*

* * *

Crossing the Desert: Learning to Let Go, See Clearly and Live Simply
(Sorin Books: 2007)

"*Crossing the Desert* offers the reader inspiration, insight, and invaluable tools for discovering the sacred presence in daily life."

Tara Brach
Author, *Radical Acceptance*

Professional Works Published by Robert J. Wicks on Resilience, Self-Care, Posttraumatic Growth, and Maintaining a Healthy Perspective

Overcoming Secondary Stress in Medical and Nursing Practice, second edition (with Gloria Donnelly) (Oxford, 2021)

Clinician's Guide to Self-Renewal, edited with Elizabeth Maynard (Wiley, 2014)

The Inner Life of the Counselor (Wiley, 2012)

Primer on Posttraumatic Growth, co-authored with Mary Beth Werdel (Wiley, 2012)

The Resilient Clinician (Oxford, 2008)

The Simple Care

OF A HOPEFUL HEART

Mentoring Yourself in Difficult Times

ROBERT J. WICKS

OXFORD
UNIVERSITY PRESS

OXFORD
UNIVERSITY PRESS

Oxford University Press is a department of the University of Oxford. It furthers the University's objective of excellence in research, scholarship, and education by publishing worldwide. Oxford is a registered trade mark of Oxford University Press in the UK and certain other countries.

Published in the United States of America by Oxford University Press
198 Madison Avenue, New York, NY 10016, United States of America.

Library of Congress Cataloging-in-Publication Data
Names: Wicks, Robert J., author.
Title: The simple care of a hopeful heart : mentoring yourself in
difficult times / Robert J. Wicks.
Description: New York, NY : Oxford University Press, [2022] |
Includes bibliographical references and index.
Identifiers: LCCN 2021016358 (print) | LCCN 2021016359 (ebook) |
ISBN 9780197515402 (paperback) | ISBN 9780197515426 (epub) |
ISBN 9780197599976
Subjects: LCSH: Mentoring. | Self-perception. | Resilience (Personality trait)
Classification: LCC BF637.M45 W53 2021 (print) |
LCC BF637.M45 (ebook) | DDC 158.3—dc23
LC record available at https://lccn.loc.gov/2021016358
LC ebook record available at https://lccn.loc.gov/2021016359

DOI: 10.1093/oso/9780197515402.001.0001

9 8 7 6 5 4 3 2 1

Printed by LSC communications, United States of America

For Brendan Geary

A true renaissance person whose wisdom comes from combining a depth of knowledge with true humility. His compassion arises from realizing the need for creativity and faithfulness to what and who in life are good. What more can you ask of a human being than this?

Do not believe that he who seeks to comfort you lives untroubled among the simple and quiet words that sometimes do you good. His life has much difficulty and sadness and remains far behind yours. Were it otherwise he would never have been able to find those words.

—Rainer Maria Rilke
Letters to a Young Poet

If everything around seems dark,
look again,
you may be the light.

—Rumi

You can either make yourself miserable,
or make yourself strong,
the amount of work is the same.

—Carlos Castaneda

Contents

Making the Most Out of Our Current Reality

A friend of mine does group work with older clients whose main challenge is being frozen by their negative attitudes toward life. He describes them as persons "waiting patiently for the past to change."

During the recent pandemic, many people spent most of their time focusing on the past and asking when we will return to "normal." Naturally, we all want this to be framed in a way that sounds sensible, so we call it "the new normal." Yet, wishing that this will be possible as a way to experience the immediate "benefit" of denial—avoiding something unpleasant—won't help us make the most out of the present time or help us be creative in planning for what's to come next. Simply fantasizing about a complete return to what life was like before experiencing a crisis or stressful events is just like sitting around waiting for the past to change. It won't happen.

Making the most of our present new way of living and seeking to prepare as much as possible for the options moving forward may not be as much fun as nostalgic longing or waiting for "the new normal." But making the most out of our current reality will make for a better future and this can be achieved by carefully mentoring yourself.

Hopefully, we can begin to do this, not in the spirit of resignation for what we've lost, but with a sense of gratitude for *good news in the making*.

Introduction

Good News in the Making

Mentoring Yourself in Difficult Times

> It is a good thing to have all the props pulled out from under us occasionally. It gives us some sense of what is rock under our feet, and what is sand.
>
> —Madeleine L'Engle

> The best teachers are those who show you where to look, but don't tell you what to see.
>
> —Alexandra K. Trenfor

C. S. Lewis pointed out that "hardships often prepare ordinary people for an extraordinary destiny." Yet, if this is to happen, there is a choice we must make in response to the following question:

> Will we allow our vulnerabilities and pain to lead to unnecessary suffering and feelings of helplessness or will they help us understand and entertain new questions and possibilities to enable us to become deeper as persons?

This is a *koan,* a life question, that has no right or wrong answer. How it is answered though will have a major impact on our destiny. In mentoring ourselves, which is designed to help us lead a richer resilient life and set the stage for greater compassion for others, the gate all of us must walk through is *vulnerability.* If we do this the right way, the results can be amazing even when, *especially* when, life becomes difficult and those around us seem lost.

When my daughter was only 8 years old she was diagnosed with severe scoliosis. This resulted in her having to wear a hard ortho-plastic cast, 23 hours a day, for 3 years. After that, because the curvature suddenly became worse even before her growth spurt, she needed immediate surgery to fuse 13 levels of her spine and have a steel rod inserted for support. After the surgery was over, people would often ask me, "Is she better?"

This is a kind and natural question. My wife and I were grateful for their concern for our daughter, as well as for how both of us were taking in all of this.

However, life is not *acute.* Everyone in life doesn't simply have one severe issue, conquer it, and then all is fine for the remainder of their lives. Life is actually *chronic.* By this I mean we must deal with small and profound challenges during our *entire* life span. My daughter's condition had acute episodes but she will need to work with the effects of her physical condition in an ongoing way for the rest of her life.

Some of us face more than others in life. That is obvious if we look around. But even more important than what we encounter is *how* we face the unexpected stress and traumas that come our way, no matter how small, large, or extensive they may be. Small stresses derail some people, while catastrophes lead others to become even more compassionate individuals who learn to live a more meaningful life in ways that paradoxically couldn't have happened had the hardship not occurred in the first place.

In my daughter's case, she didn't simply face the challenge of the surgery and then everything was all right for her. Instead, she had pain during her college years causing her at one point to crawl from her car into the house because she couldn't walk. She also almost died after giving birth to her second child. Later on, she developed breathing problems and most recently was hospitalized for a 1-day procedure and wound up spending the whole week there.

Yet, while we usually don't have a choice in many instances as to what darkness will befall us, we do have a say as to how we will deal with what we experience. How we respond to crises, trauma, severe stress, pandemics, riots, and even small disappointments or discomforts will determine who we will be and become as people. The challenges that befall us can lead us to feelings of self-pity, anger, depression, debilitating anxiety, and numbness. Such reactions are quite normal and understandable. Still, while life can be very tough for us to deal with, dark times need not be the last word. Instead, they may actually turn out to be the beginning of a new life of exploration, depth, meaning, and greater compassion.

If we acknowledge and do not play down the pain we encounter in life, on the one hand, and are also open to where it can lead us as persons, on the other hand, a form of what is now referred to as "posttraumatic growth" can occur. When this happens, we don't simply bounce back from stress, as nice as that would be. Instead, we also set the stage for becoming deeper as persons in ways that would not have been possible *had the trauma or stress not happened in the first place.* This not only has positive consequences for us but also has a positive impact on the level of compassion we are able to have for others.

In my daughter's case, one of the prominent signs she had opened herself up to such growth became very evident to me when she surprised me with a confession and expression of determination during her undergraduate college years. One morning, while we were having breakfast together, she said, "You know Dad I never told you this before but I always wanted to be a U.S. Marine Corps Officer like you were years ago." The look of surprise on my face made her laugh. She knew she had gotten the intended effect from sharing this with me so early in the morning before I had finished a second cup of coffee.

When I finally caught myself, I said, "*You did?*"

She responded, "Yes, I did but I knew I couldn't physically do it since most of the levels of my spine were fused."

"Well, what are you going to do about this desire then?" I asked.

She looked at me, smiled again, and said very firmly, "I am going to be a social worker and work for the Veterans Administration to help those who have served and are in trouble because of the horrors they have encountered."

Naturally, I beamed because she had not let the obstacles she had faced crush her desires but instead was transforming them into a role that was truly meaningful. As a matter of fact, because of what she had dealt with in her own life, my belief and hope at the time was that she would be able to respond to those who were suffering in ways that I couldn't because I had not experienced what she had in life.

Later on, she related to me an interaction she had that, to my mind, bore out my earlier hopes. She was at her desk and they had brought back someone who was in both terrible psychological and physical shape after a tour in Afghanistan. When she heard the knock at the door, looked up, and saw the discouraged face on a military veteran she had not met before, she smiled broadly at him as he stood in the doorway and asked him to come in. When he saw this welcoming look, he said, "Boy, you seem full of good energy."

In return, she told me she looked him straight in the eyes and responded, with a deep spirit and knowledge of suffering that I couldn't muster even in my best moment because I hadn't been through all the suffering she had, "You've served our country well. Now, you come on in and let us know what we can do for *you*." Needless to say, Dad was and remains proud of the woman his little girl has become.

As the previous story illustrates, one of the royal roads to resilience, and a true appreciation of humanity's need for empathy and compassion, arrives when we learn not to waste energy on denial or seek to run away from the reality of our own vulnerability. People who realize their own mortality, dependence on others, and the realities of the many unexpected changes and challenges in life are recognizable by their humility, openness, and non-defensive response to life as it is. As a matter of fact, to assume or act as if we were invulnerable can be costly. Whereas, how we live with the givens of loss, interdependence, sickness, chance, and inevitable undesirable surprises can determine the quality of our life . . . as well as the lives of those around us.

Hiding our weaknesses or pretending we are invincible not only affect how we feel about ourselves but also can impact how we welcome others with their own shortcomings and limits. To quote the poet David Whyte from his book *Consolations*:

> To run from vulnerability is to run from the essence of our nature, the attempt to be invulnerable is the vain attempt to become something we are not and most especially, to close off our understanding of the grief of others . . .
>
> To have a temporary, isolated sense of power over all events and circumstances, is a lovely illusionary privilege and perhaps the prime and most beautifully constructed conceit of being human . . .

> The only choice we have as we mature is how we inhabit our vulnerability.

Vulnerability is difficult to deny in today's world except through extreme measures such as

- idolizing power we don't have;
- excusing our aggression and hostility toward those different from us;
- looking to pharmaceuticals and science as a curtain to pull between us and loss or personal mortality; and
- embracing extreme narcissism as a way to ward off criticism.

The truly psychologically and spiritually strong among us are neither all-powerful nor persons with glossy images. They are the ones who don't deny or minimize their faults and vulnerability, on the one hand, or become paralyzed by their shortcomings or deny their true gifts, on the other hand. Neither do they take the "middle ground" and simply *resign* themselves to their fate as can be heard in an older person who proclaims with an air of discouragement: "These are not the golden years; they are the rusty ones."

Instead, the resilient among us are the ones who know and *accept* they are vulnerable in so many ways. Such an acceptance doesn't lead to their being frozen with fear. It helps them appreciate the value of letting go and honoring the fact that our knowledge is limited. They face the reality that mistakes and failures are a natural part of life—but need not trigger defensive or retaliatory action as we hear reflected in the justification of aggression as, "He only gives as good as he gets."

In a reflection on the writings of Dutch psychologist and spiritual guide Henri Nouwen, Robert Ellsberg writes,

> So often we measure our identity and success by how we remain in control. But in the end the final meaning of our lives may be determined as much by our capacity to trust, to let go, to place ourselves in the hands of another.

For some of us, that "other" was represented by a series of mentors. When such persons were absent or were toxic, we paid for it dearly. A number of years ago, I was sitting in a colleague's office chatting with him about an article that was published in *The New Yorker* magazine. It was on psychoanalysis, and we both found it fascinating and, at times, humorous. But then came a surprising turn of events. There was a period of silence in which we were obviously reflecting on both the article and our conversation up to this point and then my friend began to share both his thoughts and feelings in a way I hadn't heard him express them before.

"You know, once I finished reading the article I actually filled up emotionally and cried a bit."

This response certainly caught me off guard—not simply because of its content but also because of how he shared it. I could see he was visibly emotional now as he revealed to me that something had happened in his reading of the article that hadn't struck me in the same way. So, I waited and allowed him to amplify on his initial comment.

Once he seemed to get ahold of himself, he added,

> When the writer shared his feelings about the death of his analyst, I thought of my own losses. But what I think was most poignant for me was how it reminded me that I had not received the mentoring I felt I needed, or at least *desired* in my life.

He then went on to say,

> I'd been in my own personal psychotherapy. As a young psychologist, I had been clinically supervised on my cases. Yet, I felt what I lacked was a wisdom figure, someone with whom to share my hopes, desires, and life in a natural way.

His words at that moment brought me back to a fortuitous event in my own life. I had been attending a lecture on the contemplative, forward thinker, monk, and writer, Thomas Merton. One of the two persons delivering the presentation was Flavian Burns, Merton's final abbot before he died. He struck me as the type of mentor I had been seeking for many years. In the way he was handling questions and comments, I could see that he was welcoming, bright, a true listener, and not someone pushing an individual agenda of his own. The thought occurred to me, "Since I walked with others in darkness, should I not have someone to walk with me on a regular basis, not simply when I felt in crisis myself? I wonder if he would consider being a mentor to me?"

The thought didn't leave me for days, so I took this as a sign to act on it. I wrote him, telling him a bit about myself, and asking if he would consider meeting with me for mentoring. He responded almost immediately with an invitation to come in and speak with him about it. I did, it went well, and the mentoring relationship lasted until his death.

My friend's reaction and my opportunity to act are actually not surprising today. Due to the mobility of society, the often paucity of senior, wise family members, and the absence of structured mentoring in most professional and business settings, many people feel deeply the need for a welcoming ear, guidance, and some encouragement in today's anxious world. This absence can be sensed dramatically in the following words of minimalist poet Robert Lax when he encountered a sage:

> I feel sure that what held me about Bramacari was not so much his ideas . . . but his personality, and the kind of civilization—the kind of planet—he came from . . . as though I had always felt there must be that kind of planet somewhere and I was glad to see a representative of it come our way at last.

Receiving such mentoring can also lead to being in the position of returning the favor to others, if asked. In the case of Robert Lax, there were many others who turned to him as he entered the latter part of his life on the isle of Patmos. In one book on his conversations with Lax, Steve Georgiou, in *Way of the Dreamcatcher*, writes,

> Already in my thirties, I was at a point of transition and sought a role model who could teach me how to age well, and not grow 'old.' I needed a guide, a sage to help me in my soul searching or at least give me the confidence that a harmonic sense of balance in this life could be personally attained and shared with others.

The fact that this did occur for Georgiou is marked at the end of the book when he concludes, "I remember how after spending long evenings with Lax, I would leave the hermitage and feel as though I had landed on earth for the first time."

But the issue of mentorship mustn't stop there. Just as in the case of a therapist, it is not embracing the person of the therapist that is crucial. It is having the presence of such a person launch us on our own journey of mentoring *ourself* that matters.

After my own experiences of receiving mentoring had ended, I believed if I wished to take the next step, and mentor or guide myself each day, I would need to put similar aims forward for myself. Of course, in doing this, I knew full well that they were simply goals, not realities, given my own limited talents and present "growing edges" (defenses, anxieties, rigidity, unexplored gifts, minor signature strengths, and resistance to change) as a person. They included the following:

- Balancing gentleness with clarity in the questions asked of me—especially those that touched upon areas in which I am unsure, defensive, or sensitive about
- Providing the mental setting for me to experiment with new thinking and to find essential truths upon which to base my life more securely
- Demonstrating faith in myself even when I fail and resist insight and change
- Allowing myself the psychological space to "speak to think" rather than feel everything I recognize has to be thoroughly thought out first
- Encouraging myself to be myself by not fearing rejection or ridicule
- Helping myself recognize that having a healthy perspective is key in facing and learning from difficult times. In the end, *it is not the amount of darkness in the world or me that matters, but how I stand in the darkness with as healthy a perspective as possible*
- Not asking myself to emulate my role models by merely impersonating them but to have a sense of authenticity and ordinariness that give me the courage to "simply" be myself
- Offering a broad approach to searching further when I am lost so that I don't seek someone else's answers but seek the tools in mentoring myself to find my own responses
- Having the sensitivity to appreciate my sense of "lostness" when it occurs because what I thought I knew is no longer sufficient to the situation

We will know if we are taking these steps in the best way possible because we will

- begin to sound and behave more in accordance with beliefs we have examined rather than what the world is saying is valuable or true;
- seek to find, enjoy, and share *all* of our signature strengths—not only the obvious ones;

- catch ourselves when we only emphasize the negative feedback we give ourselves and play down the gifts we have been given that others are grateful for;
- be able to listen to criticism but be discerning in how we embrace and grow from it; and
- know mentoring ourselves is an *never-ending* pilgrimage in living life to the fullest in the short time that we have to live with meaning, compassion, and gentle joy in this world.

Fifty themes or "lessons" for reflection are presented in the chapters that follow. They are designed to prime "the psychological and spiritual pump" to reflect on your thinking, emotions, actions, and attitudes. They are purposely brief given how busy most people are today. The book concludes with a brief epilogue titled "You're Stronger Swimming Upstream" and an Appendix containing a "Month of Minute Reminders." This closing material will also help you "mentally lean back" from the current toxic culture, with its often unhelpful values, as a way to regain inner strength and even enable you to draw from often unrecognized and unexplored sources of resilience and self-respect amid difficulties, uncertainty, and a sense of personal vulnerability.

To be sure though, embracing such themes and values as vulnerability, kindness, alone time, understanding, and the others discussed has a cost. That is certain. They may not play well with some of the ways you are now viewing yourself and the world—especially during times of stress, trauma, pandemic, or even simple discomfort. However, they also promise and can deliver a sense of resilience that is to be found nowhere else. Again, the choice is up to you. *The Simple Care of a Hopeful Heart* is meant as a strong encouragement to *go for it!*

A Note on the Lessons to Follow

A number of years ago, a person whom I was mentoring said to me, "At the end of our last meeting, you said something to me that I knew you felt was important. And so, I spent a good deal of time thinking about it."

Her comment caught me off-guard so I asked, "How did you know that I felt it was important?"

In response, she laughed, and said, "You always lean forward a few inches in your chair when you speak about something you want me to take to heart."

Now, it was my turn to laugh. When I quickly thought about it, she was right.

In the brief chapters to follow, there are themes that I think are particularly important to reflect upon. You will be able to tell by the fact that I bring them up more than once. I try to focus on them from different angles so they receive the attention I feel they deserve. When you do notice this, that's me leaning forward in my chair as I sit with you.

1

"Hold on for the Next Supply"

> The fishermen know that the sea is dangerous and the storm terrible, but they have never found these dangers sufficient reasons for remaining ashore.
>
> —Vincent Van Gogh

I remember encountering a young colleague who came in to discuss a psychotherapy patient she was treating. She looked fatigued and almost sad, so I said to her, "Before we get into the case you wanted to discuss, how are you doing? You look drained."

In return, she got teary and said in a quiet, hoarse voice, "I think my soul is tired."

In response, I smiled slightly, leaned back, and said, "Well, we can't have that, can we. Why not tell me what has been going on over the past weeks or months that strike you as particularly draining since you are normally quite positive and filled with great spirits."

She then shared with me how the persons she was treating as well as some of her colleagues, family, and friends had been angry, depressed, sarcastic, belittling, lost, and critical. Slowly, without her being aware of it, they had depleted her of the energy, faith, resilience, and spirit-filled existence she normally had. She had only become aware of it just before she came in when someone said something nasty to her, thinking it was funny.

When she was done, I let the silence sit for a while, and then I told her a story about an encounter that the monk and writer Thomas Merton had with another more senior monk. I said to her,

> Merton was walking past a day room in the monastery in which he lived. He saw an elderly monk, who had been a Trappist for over 40 years, who looked sad. When he approached the old gent he asked him if he was OK. In response the monk told him he felt down, that his spirit was low and he felt he might even be losing his faith. Rather than becoming overwhelmed by this revelation, Merton simply looked at him and said, "Brother, courage comes and goes. Hold on for the next supply."

This is a good lesson for all of us to remember when people seem to misunderstand us, say something sarcastic, are themselves depressed or lonely, and have impossible expectations as to what we should and can do for them—even at times when they are not very nice to us.

During prolonged periods of stress or even minor distress that might be caused during a pandemic or another event with an uncertain aftermath, it is good to mentally lean back. In doing this, we will have the mental space necessary to imagine a face of someone who loves and appreciates us. Pausing like this also gives us the chance to take a breath and reflect on the goodness in us and the world that some draining interactions may have temporarily blocked and remember the advice given by Thomas Merton:

> *Courage comes and goes . . . hold on for the next supply!*

2

Unlearning

> The world fears a new experience more than it fears anything. Because a new experience displaces so many old experiences.
>
> —D. H. Lawrence

Mentors through the years have cautioned me not to think that my "cup" was empty when in fact it was full of my own deeply held beliefs. The old saying, "If you think you are free . . . then you are totally lost" is especially apt in terms of mentoring yourself.

A colleague, noting this, went as far as to say to me, "Mentoring yourself is an oxymoron." That is, what I was proposing in putting self and mentoring in conjunction was self-contradictory. My response was simple: "An oxymoron opens up the right side of the brain. It is like a koan, a puzzle in which there are no right or wrong answers, but how you respond determines your future." Oxymorons, used carefully, can stimulate our creativity and spirit of *un*-learning.

In political discussions today, there are people who question others who hold opposing views. They say they want to know the source of a point being made. In doing this, the message they give themselves is: I am open, balanced, and seeking new knowledge so that I can be someone who is properly informed and an educated decider. Yet, the questions are often asked about issues even though they are aware of a mammoth amount of documented information contrary to their current stand. Such actions point to the fact that they are fairly fixed in their views based on an *unconscious emotional chord within.* As beginning students are taught in General Psychology, prejudice is not reasoned into people so it won't be reasoned out.

Our pre-existing unconscious beliefs, fears, tendencies, and perspectives are often hidden. And so, just because we say we are open to hearing others' views doesn't mean we are really open and truly listening to their answers. Instead, we are silently hearing their responses while waiting for our chance to share our point of view—one that was there all along and will remain there if we are not willing to challenge ourselves, rather than others, more directly.

I once met a man who was very bright, honest, hardworking, talented, and self-confident. Yet, as I would hear his comments and questions, I felt angry and then sad at his responses. Angry, because in our discussions he presented as though he was genuinely seeking new knowledge. Instead, he was simply honing his own arguments for what he already believed.

The sadness I felt was that while I believed he could wonderfully succeed in his life, he was missing the humility that paradoxically would carry him to greatness.

Knowing this puts me on guard during the process of mentoring myself. The more I become convinced of something, the more I need to challenge, rather than take comfort in, the positions I hold and the opinions I have of others—and especially of *myself.* Mentoring ourselves and our reflection periods are based on a quite simple tenet:

> When you take knowledge and add humility, you get wisdom. And, it is that very wisdom which enables us not only to fathom our own lives but to become truly compassionate toward others as well—especially during difficult times.

Our learning never ends. I remember seeing a cartoon of a mother speaking to her daughter on her first day of school. In it she asks, "Did you learn a lot on your first day of school?" To which her little girl responds, "Yes, but they still want me to come back tomorrow."

If we understand the limits of the natural tendency to simply confirm our own comfortable beliefs, we will challenge them more often and remember: Self-confidence is not the same as self-righteousness, no matter how bright or committed we say we are to living a meaningful, compassionate life.

3

The Two Views . . . Both Are Real

> May your choices reflect your hopes, not your fears.
>
> —Nelson Mandela

"Look at the sky over there!" my wife said. I turned around and could immediately see what she meant. The low-hanging dark clouds were a total surprise. In the other direction where I had been looking, the sky was as blue as could be. I never expected a storm. How could I? Everything I saw up to that point was fine.

Both views needed to be real for me. If I ignored the fact that the storm was coming soon, it would only result in me getting needlessly soaked. On the other hand, to forget that the way I was looking was also a reality would be to make a blue sky dark when it wasn't. Both were real.

Today, during the trauma, stress, crises, and the pandemic all of us faced, the same is true: Things are tough and scary . . . but they are also filled with possibility if we have the eyes to see.

The problem is that people often find that simultaneously entertaining both realities is too difficult for them. And so, they turn their backs on one part of the situation. They either want to see things as totally dark, or at least discomforting, and speak only about that, or they involve themselves in a sense of "spiritual romanticism" by sugar-coating things and pointing only to what are possible good outcomes of the dark times.

A sign of psychological and spiritual maturity is the mental ability to hold the challenges of life in one hand and the possibilities in the other. By doing this, we are able to honor what is truly dark or dim but not be captured by it. Instead, through the eyes of gratefulness, when we hold both together in our hearts and minds, we are in an excellent position to gain a different sense of clarity. This will increase our ability to spot how unexpected darkness may cognitively shift beneficially the way in which we presently view our inner and outer worlds.

When this happens, although darkness can (and probably should) throw us off kilter in the moment (or longer!), it does allow us to view ourselves and the world in ways that would not have been possible before. The reason for this is that even though, before the darkness, we may have wanted to have a broader perspective on life, it just wasn't possible because our lives were drifting along and that is all we thought our life could hold and be.

Yet, by holding *both* realities (darkness and hope) together when situations become tough or seemingly impossible, there can be so much more in life for us. By embracing the *entire* situation both realistically and hopefully, we can set the stage to become deeper, more appreciative, helpful, and fulfilled by the new perspective that surfaces and is seen "simply" because we were looking for it!

As we mature, we learn that *how* we see something can make all the difference in whether or not we absorb new lessons in living more deeply and compassionately. Yet, to gain such a healthy perspective in the process of mentoring ourselves will take energy, commitment, and, once again at times, courage.

4

Maintaining a Healthy Perspective

Do not weep; do not wax indignant. Understand.

—William James

The Yiddish proverb, "Sleep faster . . . we need the pillows!" certainly describes what many of us feel today. The unrealistic expectations and raw emotions of others in need not only confront helping and healing professionals but also touch almost all of us who wish to be compassionate. Still, as I travel and speak on resilience, self-care, and maintaining a healthy perspective to professionals and the general public, two things strike me again and again.

First, the overwhelming needs of others arise in ways and at times that often surprise us. When I was at Dover Air Force Base, I heard that one of the volunteers working with families of the fallen was confronted by a little boy whose father in the military had lost his life in the Middle East. The little boy looked up at the volunteer as the death finally was becoming more of a reality to him and asked, "Who will play ball with me now?"

When speaking at the 92nd Street Y on my book, *Perspective: The Calm Within the Storm*, a woman of about 50 years of age came up to me after my talk and said, "I was just diagnosed with Level Four cancer, I see my surgeon this week, and am very afraid of what I will hear. Can you help me with how I feel?" Two weeks later, when I was at Notre

Dame University speaking to health care executives, one of the persons attending my presentations on maintaining a healthy perspective said to me, "You and your book on perspective have come at just the right time for me. Two months ago my 26 year-old son suddenly died."

In this era of severe stress, trauma, and uncertainty, we are faced with the pressing needs and unanswerable questions of others in different ways. Yet, there is another thing that strikes me as worth noting: that the listening space we offer others, in and of itself, is a major help.

A woman who had suffered a major sexual trauma when she was young and was seeing me as an adult showed this to me in a very simple, yet powerful, way. I asked her at the end of her therapy, "How did you get to this point? You weren't this way when you first came in to see me." In asking this, I knew that once she left therapy, she would enter darkness again at times since it comes and goes for all of us who care.

I hoped my question would provoke her bringing to mind an array of techniques she could use to face such future tough times more gently and effectively. Yet, she surprised me when she replied, "Oh, it was simple. The first time I came in to see you I simply watched how you sat with me and then I began sitting with myself in the same way." She had borrowed and learned from the respectful space she received from me.

The problem is that *we can't share what we don't have*. Unless we have an inner sense of peace, a healthy perspective, and become freer from our own sometimes exaggerated self-involvement, how can we offer space to others? And so, I have spent my whole professional life developing a list of helps with this question in mind. I enjoy presenting them in person as well as in my writings for different professional and lay groups. But the key list of some of what I think we need to remember can save a reading of these works or attending one of my presentations. They include the following:

- Having a *balanced circle of friends* who challenge, humor, and support us. Too often we settle for having friends and family who can't do this because they are unable to for some reason. A good interpersonal network can make all the difference.
- *Be faithful to being compassionate* because only being concerned about yourself will make you unhappy. When you are overly self-involved, your life will becomes too small. It is like putting a spoon of salt in a small glass—you will taste the bitterness of life. Whereas when you reach out to others, it is like putting a spoon of salt in a

lake—the bitterness dissolves amidst a wider appreciation of others' gifts and needs.

- *Healthy self-compassion* needs to sit alongside compassion for others so instead of burning out, you can enjoy keeping the flame lit for both yourself and others. Developing your own "self-care protocol/program" helps in this regard—it should be both ambitious and realistic.
- *Mentally lean back* when you feel the negative behavior, attitude, or emotions of others who are seeking to pull you in. You don't want to be callous. However, it is good to be aware that the opposite of detachment is not caring involvement, it is seduction by others' sad or angry behavior as well as their unrealistic expectations. They may not intentionally mean to behave this way. Yet, if I drop a rock on your head on purpose or by mistake . . . you still get a bump! Learn to "move your head" by leaning back from the emotions of others.

There is a lot more, of course, but I try to keep the above in mind—especially when dealing with difficult situations and people—so I thought I would share them. It helps me learn about my own large ego, have better insight into what is causing others to inflict pain on themselves, and be better able to persevere with those who have been victimized or are having difficulty opening themselves up to other points of view.

But more important, it helps me benefit as I continue my work with nonprofessionals as well as educators, physicians and nurses, psychologists, psychiatrists, counselors, social workers, members of the military, and persons in full-time ministry.

Because in reaching out to them, with the right psychological space within me, I get to see something wonderful again and again: *Good people doing great things*.

It really makes my day and inspires me to not just see only the darkness but also all the good that is going on in this world. What a blessing they are to me and my continual need to maintain a healthy perspective.

5

The Good and the Bad

Balancing Acts During Tough Times

> Healing is simply attempting to do more of those things that bring joy and fewer of those things that bring pain.
>
> —O. Carl Simonton, MD

During dark periods in our lives, it is not the amount of darkness in the world that matters. It is not even the amount of darkness in our country, religious denomination, family, or even in ourselves that matters. It is how we stand in that darkness that makes all the difference. Our perspective—how we view the world and ourselves—is key in times of crisis, and it is *balance* that determines how healthy our perspective will be.

Staying informed is good; being overwhelmed with negative information is bad. A physician at Walter Reed Army Hospital once said to me, "In a question and answer period at the hospital after your presentation, you helped me immeasurably by what you said." "What did you ask and how did I respond?" I asked. He replied, "I told you that I had come back from the battlefield and was now cutting people's legs off at the hospital and became overwhelmed when I came home, turned the TV on and felt retraumatized when the news was all negative."

And, not remembering what I said in response at the time, I asked, "Well, what did I tell you to do?" He smiled and replied, "You said, 'Well, when you start feeling that way, shut the damn thing off.'"

It is important that we stay current with what is going on with such current events as the coronavirus. To do this, checking our newspaper, becoming updated online, or watching the first few moments of the morning news is helpful. However, continuing to watch until we become swamped with a feeling of helplessness makes no sense.

Being compassionate is good; ignoring our own needs is bad. As noted previously, but can't be overstated, one of the greatest personal gifts we can share with our family, friends, and those who need our help is a sense of our own peace, resilience, and a healthy perspective on life, but we can't share what we don't have. And so, it is important to balance care for others with the space we have for ourselves. For instance, silence, solitude, and personal care—even if only for several minutes early in the morning, during a walk at lunch, or even while we are in the bathroom—are crucial for personal renewal.

Creative ways of self-care help us reach out without being pulled down. We are now very attentive to not catching the coronavirus from others. We should also be in tune with not becoming contaminated by others' sense of negativity, depressive thinking, and sense of helplessness. When we don't honor self-care, the odds of such "psychological and spiritual contamination" increase.

Concern is good; worrying is a waste of time and emotionally dangerous. Being concerned about reasonable ways to stay physically healthy and to help others in the process makes sense. However, free-floating anxiety or worrying only serves to dissipate the very energy we need to offer others and keep a healthy sense of perspective ourselves.

The self only has so much energy. If we empty our psychological reservoir, we set ourselves up for not being able to see things clearly and so are not able to remain in a position to help others. Focusing on what we have power over, and what we don't, can help us remain resilient and helpful during a time of crisis.

Emphasizing the positive is good; being involved in public relations that is not based on facts is not. Many of us hear what is good in a whisper and the bad as thunder. Those in the media and government who help us surface what is good during a crisis help us avoid focusing solely on what is dark in our lives at present. However, those who spread positive information that is not based on facts offer false hope that will in turn lead us to feel betrayed by those we should be able to trust.

Having a philosophy/ethic of meaningful living, a deep sense of faith in someone or something larger than ourselves, is good; expecting religion to protect us from pain is misguided. When we believe in God, or in a philosophy centered on leading a meaningful life such as Buddhism, we have an excellent orienting point in our lives—especially when times are tough. In areas of Syria during the war, if the residents drove at night they couldn't use their headlights because it would raise the odds of their being bombed; they had to count on a GPS.

In a crisis or other time when it is emotionally dark for us, we can still move around if we have a "psychological and spiritual GPS" of faith in some belief that is bigger than ourselves; such a philosophy cradles us emotionally. The problem is when we put such faith in others simply because they are religious leaders or spiritual guides. This is unfair to them because they are also human and may function out of their own fears, anxieties, angers, or possible narcissism. It also confuses religion and faith, which are two very different things.

Having a circle of friends to check in with is good; having an imbalance in such a group of friends is bad. In our interpersonal network, it is important to have four types of friends: the *prophet* who asks what inner voices are guiding us; the *cheerleader* who is supportive, sympathetic, and thinks we are wonderful; the *harasser* who teases us when we are taking ourselves too seriously; and the *inspirational friend* who calls us to be all we can be while accepting us where we are. The problem is that in place of such a balanced circle of friends we often gravitate to those who simply agree with us. We must remember that we may be in the same boat and happy with the agreeable company . . . but the boat may be going in the wrong direction!

Balance in our outlook is good; denial and minimization, on the one hand, or catastrophizing, on the other hand, makes no sense. During the pandemic crisis, for instance, the way to encourage an even-keeled view of the situation, others around us, and even ourselves is a simple, but often forgotten, process. When we are distressed, we need to pick up our emotions, look at how our cognitions (ways of thinking, perceiving, and understanding) have caused these feelings, and challenge ourselves to see things more clearly and accurately about what we are facing and how it can lead us to be deeper as persons (what is called today a version of "posttraumatic growth"). Our psychological and spiritual health may depend on whether we mentor ourselves with a combined spirit of gentleness and clarity or we simply let ourselves drift through crises mindlessly or anxiously. Moreover, balance can help us not simply to bounce back from stress but also to become better persons because of the way we are facing it.

6

Necessary Bump in the Road

Be like a postage stamp—stick to one thing until you get there.
—Josh Billings

When I was training to be a U.S. Marine Corps officer, each day we ran the "hill trail." It was fairly arduous and I still remember the leader having us sing as we jogged, "There ain't no sense in looking down. There ain't no gold bars [which you received if you were promoted to second lieutenant] on the ground."

I quickly learned that just beyond halfway most of us would get tired and some become stragglers. This was bad because if you received too many "straggler chits," as they were called, you ran the risk of being dropped out of the officer's training program. And so, when we would reach just beyond halfway, I taught myself to maintain my speed even though my thighs felt like someone was putting a knife in them and I felt I was running out of breath. The reward: no straggler chits.

During a modified quarantine, as happens in a pandemic or another type of limitation resulting from a dark situation in our lives, we will eventually reach a halfway point. It is at that juncture that people are tempted to take chances, feel frustrated, become grumpier, and are more apt to become anxious or glum. Being inactive or involved in unexpected draining pursuits such as home schooling or having different, abnormal eating and drinking patterns can take a toll. (A friend told me that if the COVID-19 quarantine restrictions didn't end soon, she was going to turn into a "fat person who eats and drinks too much.")

And so, during any prolonged stressful period, we need take extra care to

- remain careful in what we do and how we react because we become physically and psychologically tired after a long period in which our schedule has been radically changed;
- look at what good things have arisen that never would have happened had this quarantine or a seriously limited schedule not been imposed;
- credit yourself for doing so well so far;
- begin planning for the future when it will be over; and
- develop a healthy perspective about the many good people and things already in our lives since it is natural to forget their importance when life is moving along in a routine way.

Those of us who have had the privilege to serve in the poor areas of this country or overseas know that much of what we complain about are "First-World problems." They may be annoying, painful, or discouraging and deserve our attention. However, they are *not* the last word in life. In addition, during difficult times, if we don't mentor ourselves to navigate psychological and spiritual "bumps" in the road, well, we raise the odds that we may

- fail to learn more about ourselves and life;
- miss the chance to become more deeply grateful for the life we presently have; and
- even run the risk of illness, death, and passing on stress or, in the case of a virus, a physical illness to others.

Here comes another bump! You can navigate it if you care enough and reflect before quickly reacting in a way you might later regret.

With a little more attention to how you mentor yourself, you can raise the chances of making the most of difficult times that certainly no one would welcome under normal circumstances. New rewards you never dreamt of may be there for you if you do. Continue to be patient and go for it!

7

During Uncertain Times, Don't Miss the Opening

A number of years ago, a well-known writer and wisdom figure asked to see me. When she came in, she shared that she was having panic attacks, so I set up weekly mentoring sessions for her. When she arrived for her third visit, I suggested that instead of having the meeting in the office, we walk around the lake outside. My sense was that the beauty and activity while we were walking and talking together would put her more at ease so she would feel freer to let go and go deeper into what was behind her fears.

Halfway through the walk, she suddenly stopped on the path, turned to me abruptly, and asked in a hoarse voice, "Will these panic attacks ever go away?" In return, I looked straight into her eyes, smiled, and calmly replied, "Oh, without a doubt. That is not the problem." From the expression on her face, I could tell she was taken off guard. Finally, she found the words to ask, "Well what *exactly* is the problem then?" In response, I said, "The true challenge is whether, before the panic disappears, you can take advantage of the time you are feeling so vulnerable by seeing yourself and life more deeply and in new ways before things return to normal."

The same can be said about living through a stressful event such as a pandemic. People are wearing masks in grocery stores and distancing from each other, some are alone at home for long stretches of time, there is a fear of sickness and death, and families are either separated or thrown together in ways they haven't been for years. The upset is palpable and, at the time, the end may be still a ways off.

However, eventually this will happen and we will return to life in many, but not all, ways to which we have become accustomed. This will provide reassurance and that is good. Remaining in a crisis mode for too long can be debilitating. Yet, the danger in returning to a "new normal" is that we will forget what we have been taught during the crisis. This includes a profound appreciation of such basic, but often unappreciated, life-guiding insights as the following:

- Life is fragile, and we will die.
- Relationships matter.
- Simplicity can allow us to extract wonder and joy from "little" things.
- Silence and solitude can provide a setting for deeper self-understanding.
- A deep sense of faith in something, someone, or a philosophy greater than we are can be a light in the darkness to help us find a sustaining psychology of meaning no matter what happens; it can be a refreshing reservoir we experience deep within.
- A recognition of the need to question which aspects of the "new normal" we want to avoid, enhance, change, or add to, given what we learned during the crisis.

An unexpected encounter with trauma or any level of stress is deeply upsetting or, at the very least, annoying, somewhat discouraging, and disturbing to our usual way of living. Still, it is also a unique opportunity, a rare opening, to see ourselves and experience life more clearly.

The question that remains is: Will we open our eyes and hearts to not only see this now but also, even more important, see this when the crisis is over or has abated?

The choice is ours: Will we allow ourselves to simply return to a new "normal" or allow the insight gained from experiencing a sense of darkness to reorient our lives and embrace the new wisdom being gifted to us after the trauma's initial impact is over?

8

Five Simple Steps to Prevent Loss of Emotional Energy

During limits imposed by a stressful situation, or even the stay at home order imposed due to COVID-19, one can begin to feel physically lethargic because of a lack of activity. However, there is also a danger of emotional energy loss that can be limited or prevented with some simple steps.

This is important not only for yourself but also for those who count on you. Remember, once again, *the self is limited* and can be depleted, so relishing your own life and being compassionate toward others may become almost impossible if you are not careful. And so, what I suggest in the following steps to persons during a pandemic can also be applied to crises in general by switching a few words.

Step 1: While maintaining social distancing during a pandemic, for example, it is important to take a walk or two each day if possible. Depression and activity do not like to live together. Also, remember to take a walk and don't "take a think." By this, I mean when walking, instead of reflecting on a past you would like to forget or are nostalgic about, or dreaming of the future ("When will all of this be over?"), stay in the present and enjoy whatever you encounter instead of walking around in a "cognitive envelope" (thinking and being "all in your head" but not experiencing who and what is in front of you).

Step 2: Have low expectations and high hopes of those in your circle of family and friends. During stressful times, people say and do some crazy things. For instance, for some, the projection of blame onto those who believe or look differently than they do is a typical psychological defense mechanism. And so, some people you know will use such blaming as a way to deal with uncertainty, fear, and the fact that those they trusted are failing them and they can't admit that. Responding to such projections, rather than ignoring or blocking them, will only waste your valuable emotional energy.

Step 3: Reasonable "media distancing" is also essential—not because they are necessarily distorting the truth but, rather, because the focus is often on the spectacular and the negative rather than being balanced. Five minutes of the morning news keeps you updated; any more than that can be unnecessarily overwhelming.

Step 4: Stay in touch with persons who are themselves balanced and don't simply focus on the negative. Negative people psychologically contaminate the atmosphere, so purposely seeking out such an environment makes no sense—especially since you already have enough of such people in your interpersonal network that you can't avoid.

Step 5: Recognize what the literature on *posttraumatic growth* can teach us. It encourages us, on the one hand, to be clear about the darkness we are facing so we are not guilty of the "sin" of spiritual or psychological romanticism. Running away from, denying, or minimizing trauma and stress doesn't help. However, on the other hand, being open to seeing and experiencing the possibilities to become deeper as a person in ways that would not have been possible had the serious stress and disruption not happened in the first place can be very beneficial. All of a sudden, you may realize, as never before, the value of some quiet time, participating in a video connection with friends and family, or honoring the simple but essential joys in our brief time on this earth.

9

Taking the Little and Big Detours in Life

> We cannot solve our problems with the same level of thinking that created them.
>
> —Albert Einstein

Understanding often takes a circuitous route to finding the truth. It is not straightforward and can come via surprise, new encounters, and unexpected detours in life. Recently, I was on the way home on a route I had always taken because it was the fastest. Up ahead I could see a detour sign indicating I would need to take a circuitous route home instead of my usual one. My immediate natural reaction was annoyance. After a moment though, I realized that this was silly. I had my GPS to ensure I wouldn't get lost, and although it would take me longer, it wasn't a big deal after all.

The detour took me through a neighborhood I hadn't seen before because I would never "waste" the time to take this path home. What I saw made me smile: old houses that had carefully been restored, open fields in which children played, and large majestic trees that stood out impressively in the distance. A true graced experience made possible by my willingness to let go of annoyance so I could have the inner space for wonder.

If we think back for a moment, most of us have had and will continue to experience detours from normal life. The recent onset of a pandemic is an example of this, but all of us have many instances when this happens. One may be an occasional event, and the other is forced upon us in a way that our whole lives, and those of the people around us, are turned upside down. The question is: What can both teach us?

First, we don't have to worry about getting lost if we remember we have our inner GPS: a philosophy/psychology of living or a faith orientation. Second, if we don't focus on the deprivations, we can experience *kenosis*, the emptying of ourselves. When this happens, we don't solely experience an immediate sense of annoyance, delay, or sacrifice but also quickly find ourselves open to more . . . *much, much more.*

So, how can we enhance kenosis (a space within that allows for new experiences) rather than standing outside this open door to new psychological and spiritual awakenings? Well, we need to be clear that daily pressures because of our involvement in life, and certainly when significant negative or traumatic events occur, are certainly *not* welcomed as experiences we may desire for ourselves. To do so would be a journey in foolishness. Life is tough enough without seeking to make it more difficult for ourselves!

However, when we voluntarily embrace the natural stresses of involvement personally and professionally, and not deny the difficulties and serious dangers presented by a crisis, we can let it empty us of our usual expectations of life. We can stop mindlessly running toward our grave by being a victim of habit. Instead, we can *wake up* to the new and creative ways in life that traveling psychological and spiritual detours can provide if we welcome them with a sense of intrigue.

The key is *how* we travel life's detours. Will it be with nostalgia—simply looking back at how life was before sacrifice and change? Will it be by projecting ourselves into the future—when will all of this end? Or, will we travel with a sense of being present in the now so, like me on my physical detour driving home, we can realize there is so much we often miss because of embracing habit, speed, and expediency.

Wouldn't it be better to be open to experiencing a different "interior neighborhood," which offers so much more, *if* we have the GPS of a philosophy/psychology of life or faith tradition to guide us? With a wisdom tradition to mentally stand upon, we can take some quiet time for reflection within a period set apart to mentor ourselves by asking: What is life offering me *now* in my encounters with both daily challenges and the dangers of dramatic events beyond my control? To a great extent, the answer to that question is found within each one of us.

It is also the primary reason why taking quiet time for reflection as part of the mentoring process is so crucial.

We leave space in our schedule for so many other things. Why not for something that will guide our day and life—especially when we are living in uncertain and difficult times?

10

The One Word We Need in Really Stressful Situations

Long before psychology and psychiatry embraced the essential value of having the right *perspective*, wisdom figures of many religious traditions emphasized it. In the Talmud, we learn that we do not see things as they are . . . we see things as *we* are. In the Christian New Testament, in Matthew 6:22, it is written, "If your eye is good, your whole body will be good." Buddhists speak about it as the "unobstructed vision" and Hindus in the Upanishads as a "turning around in one's seat of consciousness." We even sense it behind comments of religious teachers through the ages. For instance, the prophet Mohammad is purported to have said at one point, "If you have enough money to buy two loaves of bread, buy only one . . . and spend the rest on flowers."

A healthy perspective does a number of things to help us avoid unnecessary suffering and to embrace the joy and support around us. In other words, it is a royal road to resilience. It does this by alerting us to pick up our emotions so we can stop, reflect, and review our thinking, which can become distorted in a crisis. One example of this is reacting in extremes. Some see stress, unexpected challenges, and pandemics occurring and panic; others fall into a sense of minimization and denial, while still others begin projecting the blame onto some thing or person outside themselves.

Another temptation is to fall back into the silver casket of nostalgia or to project into the future without doing anything in the present. In contrast, a sense of mindfulness (being in the present with your eyes wide open to seeing what is happening now) is a key to a healthy perspective.

A healthy perspective also doesn't deny the tough times in life. Instead, it faces them directly with the understanding that it is not the amount of darkness in the world or even in ourselves that matters; it is how we stand in that darkness that is crucial. And so, it is worth the effort to enhance a healthy perspective by taking a few simple but significant steps during self-mentoring.

First, anytime you have a powerful emotion (either negative or positive for that matter), ask yourself what you were thinking and believing that produced such a reaction. What often passes for common sense is actually common nonsense that has not ever been recognized or challenged.

Second, see what is in your control and what isn't so you can expend your energy on the right things because the self is limited.

Third, while not denying negative events in life or playing them down through psychological or spiritual romanticism, be open to how the situation can call you to become deeper as a person. This is known broadly in the literature now as "posttraumatic growth." A simple example is that in being open to the possible new wisdom you may gain during a crisis, you may also find that you are now more in tune with the fragility of life. Accordingly, you may then stop rushing to your grave while thinking you will live forever. The increased silence and solitude of being at home for greater lengths of time (as in the case of a pandemic, for example) may also give you the space to enjoy being with yourself more, increase appreciation for the friends you have, and make you value the need to reflect on what is truly important in life—instead of what society is trying to convince you is important.

Such stresses as those caused by trauma and pandemics are horrible and, of course, shouldn't be made light of. Make no mistake about this. However, when they do occur, the darkness they bring, once again, need not be the last word. Instead, paradoxically, such times may actually offer the *first* step in seeing and living life in positive ways that would not have been possible had the trauma not happened in the first place. Closing your eyes to this positive potential won't make the tragedy any less, but it will have you miss its possible hidden benefits going forward. And, that would be an added loss rather than a new benefit given the negative events you and I must go through at times in life.

11

Only 2 Minutes??? No Way! Yes, Way!!!

> Happiness is a butterfly which when pursued, is always just beyond your grasp; but which, if you will sit down quietly, may alight upon you.
>
> —Nathaniel Hawthorne

Recently, as a "resiliency psychologist" and former U.S. Marine Corps officer, I spoke at Ramstein Air Force Base to 2,000 airmen and they streamed my presentations into Turkey and the Azores because the U.S. Air Force was experiencing a 40% increase in suicides over their last worst year. Also, in the not too distant past I spoke in Haiti as well as in Beirut to helpers from Aleppo, Syria, who came there so I could speak to them through an Arabic interpreter. The topics were resilience, self-care, and maintaining a healthy perspective. The presentations were based on my three books, *Night Call*, *Bounce*, and *Perspective*

Without fail when I spoke to these groups about taking time in silence, solitude, and wrapped in gratitude for 2 minutes, I got the question: "Only 2 minutes? Aren't I supposed to mediate for at least 20 minutes?" To which I would respond, "Well, how long are you doing it now? It is not length of time that is important to keep a sense of a healthy perspective in life . . . it is *a regular rhythm of mindfulness*."

They would then often respond, "Oh, OK, I'll try it," to which I would say, "Oh, no! This is not a nicety. Taking out some brief quiet time to center yourself in the morning and during the day is the major portal to living a rich and meaningful life." Once again, I was trying to alert them to a main thesis of self-reflection, mentoring, and the heart of this book that is certainly touched upon by my other previous Oxford University Press works:

> It is not the amount of darkness in the world or yourself that matters . . . it is how you stand in that darkness that matters and only periods of mindfulness will open that psychological door.

Anne LaMott, in a way that only she could frame it, said, "Most things will work again if you unplug them for a minute . . . including you." But then she also wisely added knowing how we greet ourselves during periods of alone time, "My mind is like a bad neighborhood. I don't like to go there alone."

The *way* we experience quiet time is important. Otherwise, during our quiet time we will create a mental vacuum. And, since nature abhors vacuums, the preconscious—that area that lies just beyond our daily level of awareness—will rise up into our consciousness. We will then see what we have sought to bury. The result? To protect ourselves, we will stop being mindful. In response, the suggestions I make here, as I do to the groups to which I present, are that when we quietly reflect, we need to

- be nonjudgmental and act as if our thoughts and feelings that arise are those of someone else so we can see them clearly with a minimum amount of defensiveness and learn about the erroneous judgments that are running around in our minds without our being clearly aware of them (remember that the only memory that will hurt you is the one totally forgotten that continues to influence what you believe without you knowing it!);
- neither entertain nor suppress any thought that comes up but instead let it move through you like a passing train that leaves new self-understanding about yourself instead of merely the psychological blemish of self-blame; and
- return to a gentle image within, refocus on some object in front of you, or return to a mantra such as "gentleness" or "compassion."

And so, what is the bottom line? Approach quiet time with a sense of intrigue and gentleness. Give yourself a break to help avoid wasting time and energy on others who are misbehaving, and embrace the good that is truly around and within you. During this "2 minutes," and hopefully eventually longer periods of time, gratefulness for who you are and what you already have, will serve to open your eyes further to what you are missing that is also already around you to enjoy. In addition, you will learn more about what you have absorbed in life that is both inaccurate and, in the end, dysfunctional. Not a bad deal, eh?

12

Change and Loss

> I like living. I have sometimes been wildly, despairingly, acutely miserable, racked with sorrow, but through it all I still know quite certainly that just to be alive is a grand thing.
>
> —Agatha Christie

Writer Kathleen Norris, in her book *Dakota*, said with respect to change, "Disconnecting from change doesn't recapture the past, it loses the future." As ancient Eastern philosophies also remind us, the only constant in life is change—and unfortunately that includes loss. In a situation of loss, the more significant the person or object lost, the greater the difficulty and longer it takes to adjust. Change and loss both require a sense of recognition of the impact, an ability to express one's emotions about the loss, a need to alter one's life accordingly, and, finally, an ability to put who or what was lost in a new place in one's life.

I remember a woman once coming to me regarding what she thought was a prolonged grieving process. She told me that friends and neighbors told her she shouldn't keep so many photos of her husband around the house but she had difficulty taking them down even though others kept telling her she must let go.

I asked her how long ago he had died. She replied that it has been about a year. In response, I smiled and said, "Oh, is that all? Was the relationship a good one?" I then asked. "Yes, it was wonderful."

And I responded,

> That's great. So many couples don't have the relationship you have had. And, by the way, the answer is not in letting go of him. You probably won't ever let go of him since he played such a significant and positive place in your life. Instead, when you feel ready, he will take a different place in your life.

Then, I pointed to my chest and said, "He will always be with you in your heart but in a different way."

When she came back the next week to see me, she had an impish smile on her face. I asked her about the expression and she said, "I took all the photos down except the one by my bedside." In return, I asked, "Well, what led to that decision?"

"I realized that I didn't ever need to let go of him. And so, I didn't need his photo all over the house because he was always with me in here," pointing to her heart.

Loss, stress, trauma, and such environmentally dramatic events as pandemics often cause irreparable changes and, very sadly, some significant losses. Over time, we will be required to accommodate these realities. In doing this, we don't deny that the loss was profound. We don't quickly move on. Yet, on the other hand, we realize that to resist recognizing that a change has occurred is futile. It is like ruminating over something that has happened while waiting for the past to change. It is not going to happen. Setting up your tent amidst life's tragedies or seeking to hold onto what you have lost is a tragedy in itself.

Instead, hopefully, we will have the satisfaction of bringing good memories of the past into our hearts and appreciate what joy they brought us as we nod to ourselves in gratitude for the privilege of having had such experiences. Then, when we can, we change our lives accordingly to make space as best we can for new experiences. There is no rush. There is no magical timeline. There is just the call to be in "the new now" in a way that honors the past and appreciates the present so we can be as open as possible to what the future might unfold.

This takes a recognition that life can never be called "fair." If we constantly look for why something happened, we will never appreciate the positive aspects of who and what are around us now. Instead, the call is to look for "love" in the world as it shows itself in different, possibly radically new, ways. In doing this, we will be in the best position to see what is good and feel both comforted and encouraged to move on.

Television's Mister Rogers once said, "When I was a boy and I would see scary things in the news, my mother would say to me, 'Look for the helpers. You will always find people who are helping.'" To this I would add, also look at the good within yourself and realize that you are part of this wonderful compassionate force in the world. This will remind you that you are not alone but, rather, part of an enduring great spirit that will always live on no matter what happens or how dark the skies may seem.

13

Feeling Lost and Making Stupid Mistakes

When unexpected crises have changed our lives, at certain points it is not unusual to experience a sense of "feeling lost" and making stupid mistakes we would normally not make in our dealings with others and life.

In my case, given my work with the prevention of *secondary* stress (the pressures experienced in reaching out to others), I deal with helping and healing professionals who work on the front line and are often in serious danger. At the other extreme are my own personal small stresses that are part of daily life.

Recently, I could tell I was sinking because a *small* irritant *totally* annoyed me. This surprised me since at the time I wasn't dealing directly with the more major issues of health care workers who were feeling a sense of guilt because they couldn't help their patients due to a lack of resources and had deep fears of bringing a contagious disease home to their families. When they were in trouble, they could count on eliciting from me patience and a willingness to enter with them into the darkness and sense of feeling lost. Yet, now, after a minor incident in my own life, I was not understanding but annoyed. During such times as these, I try to take note of myself when something in the way I handle things ends up to be hurtful, inadequate, or far from how I wanted it to go.

In response to such failings, I think all of us need to try to avoid guilt, which only pulls us into the past and leaves us there. Instead, there is a need to have genuine remorse. In this case, we learn how we have failed others in the present and seek to learn from our mistakes so we can be more understanding and behave in a more enlightened fashion going forward.

Feeling lost during a long-standing crisis, such as the recent pandemic, is natural. Acting out by doing or saying things that aren't helpful is also to be expected at times. How we deal with such personal failings, or a sense that we are lost amidst it all, is nothing to be ashamed of.

If we expect to grow from such errors, we need to take the time and space in a quiet moment to lean back from the situation, see what we can learn, and then move on so we can try to do better next time. Such steps are at the core of the process of mentoring yourself.

And so, if you are feeling lost during a crisis or stressful episode, you have a lot of company so don't feel strange, alone, or that you are less of a person. If you push what I have said further by asking, "Well, *who else* feels lost at times, handles things poorly, and emotionally responds to the little things in immature ways at times?" The answer I can offer you is simple: *me*.

You may feel lost but you are not alone. Take heart. You are doing the best you can and that is wonderful. *Learn* what you can from failures and *move on*. Dwelling on them in a negative way will only short-circuit the wisdom needed to become deeper as a person. It would be a shame to miss such opportunities for self-discovery. Always be as clear as you can be in looking at yourself, your gifts, and foibles or those "growing edges" previously mentioned that represent those areas needing further development, psychological "pruning," or correction. However, don't forget to be gentle as well.

If we solely focus on becoming clearer about how we need to improve, we will cause ourselves "narcissistic injury." By that, I mean we will only cause unnecessary personal hurt. On the other hand, if we are only gentle with ourselves, we may gloss over things and prevent personal development in areas that need attention. By combining gentleness with clarity, we can truly gain insight without unnecessary pain.

This is a balancing act that is truly at the heart of the mentoring process in general and how we view ourselves in particular. It also avoids the psychological dead ends that arise out of feeling upset over something we have done. If we can truly become intrigued about our feelings, cognitions (ways of thinking, perceiving, and understanding), and actions, we will be less apt to project blame onto others, castigate ourselves, or become unduly discouraged. A spirit of intrigue will also encourage us to take some time at the end of each day to reflect on what happened, how we felt about it, and what actions we took or avoided. It is a wonderful journey in learning about ourselves and those around us and the heart of the self-mentoring process.

14

During Tough Times . . . You Owe It to Yourself!

Given the dangers and significant upheaval being caused by the recently experienced coronavirus, delusions—especially by the "well-educated" like myself—have included such beliefs as the following:

- Scientists will cure all and they will do it *immediately*.
- Political leaders will show us the way—surely they wouldn't be partisan during a crisis.
- Economic security is here to stay.
- Physically getting together with my community is an answer I can count on.
- Religion will keep me afloat.

Whereas such basic beliefs are under stress at this time, and we feel anything from discomfort to great fear and loss, such major disruptions in our belief system can provide fresh avenues to a deeper appreciation of a more mature philosophy of life.

For one, the failure of science to provide immediate gratification and answers reminds us to appreciate that we also must do our part in taking care of the earth we have been given. Rolling back clean air and water guidelines for the sake of immediate economic gain is, dare I use the word, a "sin" that will hurt our children and grandchildren to come. Science has shown us the way in many areas and will help now, but it alone is not the answer.

Whether you are conservative or liberal in your political stance, *character* does matter. Being a person whose agendas bring us together, not tear us apart, is a cornerstone of leadership in a time of crisis. Also, leadership includes the ability to empower others. Republican President, and before that "General," Dwight D. Eisenhower once noted, "Leadership consists of nothing but taking responsibility for everything that goes wrong and giving your subordinates credit for everything that goes well."

Economic security also is an illusion. What seems certain now can be gone tomorrow. Saying, "Oh, the stock market will come thundering back in a few months" is not based on reality. Recognizing that there are such things as economic "game changers" and not obsessing ourselves with them but, rather, doing what we can to make do with what we have certainly is based on reality.

Appreciating the value of community and friendship makes sense. Expecting it will always be there *in the way it has in the past*, doesn't. Sometimes a relative or friend you love moves away or dies, or we take for granted that we can always physically meet with those from our spiritual or local community.

Finally, many of us believe that during dark times religion will buoy us up and, in many ways, it may. However, as one Christian theologian put it, "Jesus didn't call us to a new religion . . . he called us to *life!*" And so, we are called to realize that it is *faith*, not the delivery system as we know it, that is the most important factor for many of us. Religion is essential because it is the human bridge to faith. But when we forget it is only the "bridge," then we may fail to remember that it is faith, with love at its heart, that is truly essential. If we forget this, then the beauty of religion fades and it can divide us from each other and even from a Spirit of love. This may happen because we listen to others around us with similar misconceptions and fears or the preacher who yells the loudest when he knows the least.

But then when this happens, if we are open to the crisis waking us up, while we may feel no less discomfort or pain, the suffering we experience because we are holding on to an idol or psychological security blanket can be dissipated by the chance to return to such basics of life as

- an honoring of science without worshipping it and a willingness to take care of our earth;

- a recognition that all of us—especially our leaders—need to have humility in order to focus their energy on others . . . not just on themselves;
- an appreciation that we need to be grateful for what we have and share it with those less fortunate because gratitude opens our eyes to all that is *already* there which we may be missing now; and
- a renewed and deeper understanding of the importance of staying connected with others, not simply in person, but over the phone, via the internet, and, yes, even with a physical letter, card, or package sent.

And, for some of us, maybe the most important basics: an embracing of a philosophy or faith that is not based on division, hate, or feeling closer to the Truth than others because of what we believe. Instead, it is a faith in the goodness of humanity that impels us to search for how we have been led by our heroes, "scriptures," and philosophical/psychological tenets. It is also good modeling to seek new ways to be present—especially to those different than we are—because at the end of the day, we know that above all things, love is at the heart of life . . . we are all in this *together*.

15

Pacing and Timing

The Forgotten Key Factors

In supervising or mentoring mental health professionals and spiritual guides, I would occasionally ask why they said something to the person coming to them for help. Often, the response was, "It was the right thing to say. What I said was correct."

My response frequently would be,

> Well, let me amplify on my question by asking you:
>
> Why did you say that?
>
> Why did you say that *now*?
>
> Why did you say that now *in that way*?
>
> And, in saying that now in that way, *what did you expect*?
>
> In intervening with others, we must ensure we are also taking into consideration:
>
> Whether the *timing* was ideal to make such a comment
>
> How we *phrased* something
>
> And, what our *expectations* were in making such an intervention.

The same can be said when we mentor ourselves and in our decision to do something based on what we discover after examining our feelings, cognitions, beliefs, and planned actions. As most of us know from past experiences, acting when we feel either depressed or manic about something is not a good idea. A calm demeanor usually leads to more intelligent decisions and actions.

Many times we don't realize that we resist both insight and action because the timing for them is not ideal. To help with this, I often remind myself of the following when I am seeking to better understand and act upon something:

- Try to look at everything in life as if it were happening to someone else. In this way, it is possible to gain some distance from the emotions involved. This opens up neutral space to look at the events, as well as the feelings, cognitions, and beliefs we have and actions we have taken with less tendency to blame others or ourselves. When we do this, it increases the chances that we will learn more and waste less energy in self-condemnation or defensiveness.
- Recognize that nothing understood needs to be changed within a certain amount of time. Such an attitude will help us avoid feeling overwhelmed to the extent that we will feel compelled to think: "This is how I am. I will *never* change."

Mentoring ourselves is designed to help us make friends with ourselves and our resistances rather than start a personal psychological war with the way we think and act. Pacing and timing in how we approach ourselves will make the whole process of change easier and more personally rewarding.

16

Being Creative During an Extended Crisis Is Great . . . but Also Don't Forget the Basics

When I discovered how people were not simply coping but actually flourishing during COVID-19, I was excited. During this pandemic, as with other crises they faced, they continued to come up with creative methods of not only surviving lockdowns and other limitations but also becoming involved in initiating new ways of behaving, thinking, and deepening their lives in ways that were truly admirable.

However, I also encourage all of us not to forget some simple basics that we need to remind ourselves of during ongoing crises. In such situations, it is helpful if we do the following:

- Develop a new routine that is in keeping with the limits being imposed to keep us safe.
- Interact over the phone, via email, and other creative ways (Zoom, FaceTime, Skype, etc.) with people who are both positive and realistic. Those who are simply positive can be reckless in their actions because of being in a state of denial. Others who are only "realistic" can psychologically contaminate our spirit by initiating and echoing only the negative.
- Try to concern ourselves with what we can control and not worry about what we can't. On the other hand, we also need to be gentle with ourselves so if and when we do worry, we don't wind up picking on ourselves for doing it!

- Try to get some exercise each day—even if it is only walking around the house—and get some fresh air—even if it is only opening the window for a bit.
- Be compassionate and think of others. When we get outside of ourselves, it helps us keep a healthy perspective that is not possible if we are only self-involved.
- Recognize when we feel our anxiety becoming free floating and not attached to anything specific, to try to focus on *exactly* what we are afraid of. This will lead us to ask ourselves what we can do about the specific fears and help us recognize what we can't control and need to let go of.

As I noted, what I have just covered is nothing new, nothing radical, nothing creative . . . but still worth keeping in mind going forward. If mentoring ourselves isn't practical enough to keep such basics in mind, it will cease to be a dynamic process involved in enhancing a life well *lived*, not one simply thought or fantasized about.

17

Take a Break When Necessary . . . So You Can Continue to Be Involved

Persons will often tell me how overwhelmed they are by watching the morning and evening news. Since the media covers stories in the news—*especially* negative and dramatic ones—it is not unusual to hear primarily, or sometimes "only," what is horrible. Whether it is in the world and coming to our shores soon or, "better yet," in our neighborhood that is threatening, it is covered in great detail. To avoid such news is not helpful because that behavior would leave us totally in the dark. And, although that might seem like a good idea at times, and the image of living on a desert island is pretty attractive, it is helpful to keep informed so we will be better prepared.

However, as mentioned previously, there is a limit for all of us that must be respected. Otherwise, listening to the same negative story from many different angles can dispirit us. All of us should want to remain involved in difficult times. Not to be committed to what is good, is not remaining neutral; it is encouraging evil. We don't want our active concern and involvement in the right causes to cease.

However, a reality we must face is that the self is limited. And so, for us to remain committed, we do need breaks so we don't become negatively overstimulated to the extent that we start to feel helpless, become discouraged, and become drained of the energy to be compassionate.

Part of the way we can accomplish continued involvement is in being clearer on the difference between "taking a break" and "running away." When we run away, it is an effort to *permanently* escape what we *must* face. Whereas in taking a break, we recognize that refreshing and renewing oneself sometimes include giving ourselves a break for a while. When we have the humility to do this when necessary, it can make all the difference.

As previously indicated, if we pace ourselves, we will be fine. Moreover, another result of our doing this is that others will continue to benefit from our commitment to being a light in the darkness as well.

18

The "Small Things" During a Crisis and Its Aftermath

There has been a great deal of coverage of the quite serious problems that arise during a crisis such as a pandemic. Sickness, the possibility of death, financial losses, and the absence of a clear path going forward are just a few. However, the so-called "small things" that result from even being in the midst of a pandemic are important to note as well.

Lockdowns that limit movements, changes in schedules, having us put on masks, and spending much more time either alone or in close proximity to those we live with can have impacts that we often don't want to speak about. After all, health care workers are risking their lives, others are fearfully cornered in assisted living housing, and small business owners are worried about losing everything. Who are we to focus on our smaller problems?

Although this is true and good to keep in mind, being aware of a few basics is a way to

- enhance a healthy perspective;
- limit *unnecessary* complaining; and
- improve our awareness for all that we should be grateful for while at the same time recognizing that ventilating and sharing the "small things" that are tough in our own lives on occasion is still a good idea.

If we ignore or bury what we are feeling about what is going on around us, it can have a significant impact on both our mood and how we interact in a dysfunctional way with those we love as well as those whom we meet in the grocery store or other venues we venture out to visit.

And so, the following are additional things to keep in mind:

- *To monitor our mood more closely* so as not to react to others immediately. When under pressure, we want to be careful so "our mouths are not close to our unconscious." By that, I mean that we don't quickly say something we might regret later and that may hurt others unnecessarily. The approach to be considered is: When we feel something, don't immediately react. Instead, do a "double-reflection." First, reflect within ourselves as to what and why we are feeling the way we are. The first answer we give ourselves to this reflection is usually too shallow. We need to push ourselves to see what it is that is *really* causing our reaction. Others with different personalities and concerns might not respond this way. Second, if the opportunity presents itself, and it is appropriate, then reflect with the other person about what is concerning us.
- To utilize *some time and space in our schedule* that we might not normally have and seek to use it in planning how we want to live differently once the restrictions of a pandemic or limits due to another type of crisis are largely lifted. For instance, we must take the time to ask ourselves: What part of the "past normal" do we *not* want to return to? Drifting back into our former style of living may feel comfortable, but it will also waste uncovering and incorporating possible lessons in meaningful living that could only be offered during what we are going through at this point.
- As we live through these uncertain times, we should seek to develop *a new structure for our day and week* that is more in line with the changes we are enduring. Just stumbling through each day while waiting for the crisis to plateau or disappear may result in us psychologically and spiritually tripping over ourselves. An example of this is eating, drinking, and not exercising in ways that would be helpful. "Medicating ourselves" with mind- and life-numbing television or indulging in ongoing negative conversations with others over the phone or in person will also not make us feel better even though it may temporarily help alleviate a sense of loneliness since

"misery likes miserable company." However, in the long term, it will not be helpful. Instead, it will simply be a waste of the short time we all have in life.

In essence, surrounding ourselves with as many positive influences as possible also makes sense—whether it be in person, electronically, or even in what we read. If and when we have been forced to take a mini-sabbatical due to something unforeseen in life, it is foolish not to use the time as best as we can. We won't regret it. As a matter of fact, we will look back when the so-called "new normal" arrives and be able to say to ourselves, "That was truly a pain in the neck . . . but it opened me to life in ways that would not have been possible *had the crisis not happened in the first place*."

19

Planning Versus Preoccupation

Very, Very Different

Planning is a fun activity and very useful in our lives. It is a key part of mentoring ourselves that takes place in "the now." Its focus is on what we can control and how we can reasonably prepare for the future. We can tell emotionally that it is a "planning" process because during it, we are intellectually engaged and possibly even excited. When it is over, we feel a sense of accomplishment and satisfaction.

Preoccupation, on the other hand, is not discerning about what can be controlled in the future and what can't. It is also emotionally draining, not exciting, and rather than a sense of having achieved something, there is free-floating anxiety and a sense of loss of control and diminishment of hope during and after it.

This distinction is important as we look ahead with respect to a crisis or stressful situation. Focus first and foremost on what we can control. This allows us to dream about what else might eventually be possible without becoming obsessed with the thoughts about what might or not might occur.

If we do become anxious about the future and what we can't control, the simple response is to emotionally lean back and congratulate ourselves for picking up the anxiety. Following this, we must ask ourselves what is in our control and mentally list such things and possibly even write them down if this will help. Also, it is helpful if we note to ourselves what we cannot predict or control since they are not worth the effort or time spent on them.

This approach will

- lessen our anxiety;
- free up space to focus on what can be controlled;
- allow us to enjoy the present as much as possible; and
- leave creative room to develop new talents and ways to be happy given the realities of what is happening now.

You may say in response, "I don't like it! I want this crisis or stress to end!" Well, you are right. Who does like it? And so, I give you total permission to stand in front of the mirror and yell it 10 times.

You may ask, "How will such an activity help?"

Well, at the very least, if we haven't had a haircut in ages because we were too busy or because we were locked down due to a pandemic, we will see that we need to comb our hair more often because our neighbors are starting to talk about us! As one might expect, a sense of humor also helps in these difficult times.

20

Amazingly, Few Report This . . . But They Do Exist! I Have Seen Them

During the past years, I have had a chance to travel across America as well as around the world to such places as Edinburgh, Hanoi, Port au Prince, Frankfurt, London, Belfast, Sydney, Auckland, Budapest, Phenom Penh, Beirut, and Malta. The purpose was to speak on resilience, self-care, maintaining a healthy perspective, and the integration of psychology and spirituality from a world religions' perspective. I tried to collapse the key concepts in my books *Night Call*, *Bounce*, and *Riding the Dragon* and present them—primarily through stories and illustrations—in a way that the material would be practical, inspirational, thought-provoking, and helpful.

The audiences primarily were nongovernmental organizations (relief workers), physicians and nurses, clergy, members of the military, psychologists, psychiatrists, social workers, educators, and counselors—all healing and helping professionals on the line working in often impossible situations.

They were people of hope who put their best wishes into action for the betterment of the human race. They weren't people seeking to divide society, and they didn't first check a person's gender, race, religion, or country of origin before helping them. Their main problem was they were too hard on themselves and simply needed a bit of direction, encouragement, and appreciation of the balance needed among three areas: presence to others, presence to self, and presence to something (a philosophy or mission) or someone (a wisdom figure, philosopher, sage, mentor, or God) greater than themselves.

The wonderful thing is that such good people live and share of themselves all around the world—certainly in our neighborhoods, if we look for them. However, we, our neighbors, and the media rarely speak about them. Instead, only the bad news seems to get publicized and mentioned.

Well, good people *do* exist. Amazingly wonderful things are happening all around us by people we don't know—and some we do. And so, while some leaders in governments may take away poor people's food stamps and line the pockets of the rich, there are others who feed the hungry and welcome the stranger.

As a matter of fact, *you* may be one of them. If you are, thank you. Don't let the darkness discourage you. What you are doing is making a difference. It may not be loud . . . but it is a true reflection of the warmth and goodness still present in the world. Again, thank you! . . . and please bring this to *mentoring yourself* when times are tough.

21

I Must Remember That . . .

There are several simple tenets of mentoring ourselves that are more important than others. Among them, I would include the following:

Reflection must always precede reaction.
Rudeness is not the same as resilience and strength.
Gentleness is not being a doormat to evil.
Kindness to strangers doesn't mean I don't also care for people who look like me.
Welcoming the poor is a reminder that no matter how hard I have worked, *all* is a gift.
Calling people names is not defending a cause but encouraging conflict.
Being proud that I am an American doesn't mean that it is acceptable to reject or ignore the needs of those who are from elsewhere—patriotism is good; nationalism is dangerous.
Recognizing my fears is a good way for me to prevent reacting with hate.
Appropriately sharing my vulnerabilities doesn't mean I am weak.
Being grateful is a wonderful way for me to see what I already have rather than only what I want.

A sense of entitlement often masquerades as a claim that I am being treated unjustly.
Emphasizing a single good cause, while closing my eyes to others, is simplistic, not simple goodness.
Being compassionate doesn't mean that I can heal or help *everyone as they would like or demand*—even if they are from within my family or close circle of friends.
No one can go it alone but must have friends who challenge, support, tease, and inspire them.
When I am experiencing real joy and peace, instead of pleasure and comfort, it is a way others can also become more hopeful in my presence because of how I am modeling serenity.
Mindfulness meditation joins me with a living communion of compassionate people, which is pretty good company to keep in life.

Yes, there is a lot to remember in self-mentoring as a way to

- enhance our signature strengths;
- be able to share them with compassion; and
- avoid unnecessary negative or distorted thinking that would pull us down in some way.

Given the previous points, making a personally developed list of key elements and discoveries about self-mentoring, like I have done, is a good practice to embrace. Doing it results in being involved in the process of self-examination in general. It also records themes and wisdom that might be forgotten if not recorded and reviewed from time to time.

22

The Blame Game

> In the second half of life, one of our major tasks is to withdraw our projections.
>
> —Carl Jung

> How many of us have bowed our heads and said, "Lord show me where *I* am wrong?"
>
> —Anonymous

Years ago, I realized that everything negative said about me, no matter how poor the motivation of the person saying it, was true to some extent, and if I could "psychologically and spiritually mine" what they said, I would be freer. As persons such as the Dalai Lama would indicate, those who are not our fans can teach us much if we are open to learn it.

However, I also remembered the lesson of the wonderful training analyst who taught me at Hahnemann Medical College and Hospital who said, "Projection of blame is one of the most primitive defenses and if someone uses that as a primary way of defending themselves, it demonstrates they are fearful and not very mature."

And so, when I am criticized, I seek to find the truth, sometimes hidden in the criticism, because it can help me learn about myself—even if that was not the intention of the person saying hurtful or negative things. It also prunes my big ego and provides me diagnostic information about the person doing the criticizing. For some, it is the best they can do. And so, while I need to know not to retaliate, I should also recognize that I must have low expectations and high hopes as to how they can respond to any critical feedback, support, or intervention about how they are behaving, thinking, or believing.

Yet, I must confess that people who are so quick to blame me and others for their own problems can be dangerous. Not only do they deplete me but also simultaneously they may wind up emptying me of the good energy that I wish to offer others as well. It is this realization that makes me not give away the power to even those who use pure projection to protect themselves. I recognize in not giving away the power to them, it is not simply about me . . . it is about those who count on me as well. After all, we can't be all to everyone—especially those who have chosen us as their enemy because they don't have the ability to look at their own behavior.

In the novel *Kingdom of the Blind*, author Louise Penny shares the following about one of the characters in the book, Myrna, who is a psychologist:

> Holding resentments. How many clients had Myrna sat across from as they complained about having been "done wrong"? Whose grip on grievances was so tight it strangled reason. They'd give up sanity before giving up these injustices. In some cases, in some people, it went on for years and years. The thorn planted firmly in their side. And while Dr. Landers had listened, guided, made suggestions on how to try to let their pain go, still they'd let it fester, until she finally realized some clients didn't want freedom from their resentments, they wanted validation. Entitlement was, she knew, a terrible thing. It chained the person to their victimhood. It gobbled up all the air around it. Until the person lived in a vacuum, where nothing good could flourish. And the tragedy was almost always compounded, Myrna knew. These people invariably passed it on from generation to generation. Magnified each time. The sore point became their family legend, their myth, their legacy. What they lost became their most prized possession. Their inheritance. Of course, if they lost, then someone else had won. And they had a focus on their wrath. It became a blood feud for the bloodline.

Yes, we are all imperfect and don't do things absolutely right, *but* when people emphasize it too much, there is something else going on in *them* that they don't recognize. We can't afford to feed this because of our own welfare as well as the welfare of those who count on us not to give away our energy to critics who don't have the best intentions.

In his classic work *The Te of Piglet*, Benjamin Hoff helps us put this in perspective with the following enjoyable story many of us recall from years past and is worth retelling here as a way of finishing this self-mentoring lesson:

> While traveling separately through the countryside late one afternoon, a Hindu, a Rabbi and a Critic were caught in the same area by a terrific thunderstorm. They sought shelter at a nearby farmhouse.
>
> "That storm will be raging for hours," the farmer told them. "You'd better stay here for the night. The problem is, there's only room enough for two of you. One of you'll have to sleep in the barn."
>
> "I'll be the one," said the Hindu. "A little hardship is nothing new to me." He went out to the barn.
>
> A few minutes later there was a knock on the door. It was the Hindu. "I'm sorry," he told the others, "but there is a cow in the barn. According to my religion, cows are sacred, and one must not intrude into their space."
>
> "Don't worry," said the Rabbi. "Make yourself comfortable here. I'll go sleep in the barn."
>
> A few minutes later there was a knock at the door. It was the Rabbi. "I hate to be a bother," he said, "but there is a pig in the barn. I wouldn't feel comfortable sharing my sleeping quarters with a pig."
>
> "Oh, all right," said the Critic. "I'll go sleep in the barn." He went out to the barn.
>
> A few minutes later, there was a knock at the door. It was the cow and the pig.

23

Be Aware of the Dangers of Toxic Compassion

> The brighter the light, the deeper the darkness.
>
> —Carl Jung

In uncertain times, wanting to be a good friend, parent, companion, adult child of elderly parents, family member, co-worker, or any type of caring presence to those you meet is beautiful. Truly beautiful. But, it also can be very dangerous at times. The more caring we are, and the wider our circle of care, the more menacing it can be to our own psychological and spiritual well-being. Not just those in the helping professions, but also all deeply compassionate people, simultaneously put themselves in a position to live a rich meaningful life while also placing themselves in harm's way because of being so compassionate and available.

People who are suffering because of loss, neediness, disability, or trauma may inadvertently or purposely "psychologically bleed" on caring individuals who didn't hurt them in the first place. There are no winners when this happens. As the saying goes, "Blowing out someone else's candles won't make yours any brighter." But suffering people sometimes react as if it will. At times, those in distress react with the unconscious, dysfunctional belief that only when others are made to feel vulnerable will they feel better or justified themselves. In addition, in some cases, being broken is an end in itself because the person believes it will gain them attention. It is as if they erroneously believe: If I am OK, show I am grateful for the efforts being made, or improve, people will run away and no longer be by my side.

People in need can also be toxic to those seeking to help them. And so, a primary goal in remaining compassionate is not to become psychologically contaminated in a negative way by the very people at work, in our family and circle of friends, and others who think that diminishing us will increase the attention they believe they deserve in the way they believe it should be offered. As another popular saying from an anonymous source often posted on the internet also goes: "It's not your responsibility to detox toxic people. But, it is your job to decontaminate the parts of yourself that are vulnerable to their particular toxicity."

Knowing that such things like this can and do happen may make all the difference in being able to remain a continuous healing presence without being pulled down in the process. Losing a compassionate tone would be a shame if the dangers of helping others end up preventing a caring presence or end up burying our caring nature because others are unhappy with the efforts we are making on their behalf. There are already enough callous, overly self-involved and harsh persons in today's society. The presence of compassion is now needed more than ever in society given the tragedies and unwanted changes triggered by crises that may continue with us in the foreseeable future.

Professional helpers and healers realize the importance of reaching out without being pulled down. Yet, often well-meaning nonprofessionals don't. As a result, when interacting with others who are going through dark times, they fail to appreciate that they are putting themselves in a precarious position due to the exposure to psychological hurt, neediness, stress, anxiety, anger, and trauma. The situation is also made even worse if the person's long-standing personality style of dealing with the world is dysfunctional (referred to in professional psychological terminology as a "character disorder").

People who have experienced severe trauma (which unfortunately is becoming increasingly prevalent today), sudden loss, or significant disappointment can also be like a drowning swimmer. Because they fear they are losing their way or are already totally lost, they may unintentionally seek to emotionally strangle the very persons attempting to help them.

So what is the response to how we should handle the dangers of caring for others we love or whom we are in an ideal position to help? Similarly, how can we learn how to improve our style in ways that we remain compassionate without giving away our joy or own peace in the process? Finally, especially since time to educate ourselves on preventing *secondary* stress, the pressures experienced in reaching out to others, is quite limited, how can we find the space to learn what we need so we don't become even more fatigued? This is especially the case in dealing with persons in our family and circle of friends who use the psychological defense called "splitting."

Splitting occurs when a person divides people into two stark categories: "the good" and "the bad." To them, those who are "good" are persons who meet their demands in the way they want them met. Whereas the bad are those who fall short of their exact desires *now*. (With persons who use splitting as a defense, you can be good one moment and declared bad the next depending on their immediate desires and how you meet or don't meet them.)

Many years ago, a professor of mine shared an image that he used with his psychotherapy patients. He would remind them that in years past, some toilets used to have a large box on the ceiling filled with water with a chain hanging down from it. After going to the bathroom, a person needed to pull that chain to release the water in it to flush the toilet. He said,

> Picture that box but full of feces, not water, and that what you are now doing is pulling the chain while your head is under it. The answer to this is: either don't pull the chain or at least have the sense to cognitively move your head!

In toxic relationships, this is exactly what we must do. The basic problem is we often don't realize that the relationship is problematic. In such cases, although we feel badly after the interaction, we may make excuses for the other person: "Oh, they really didn't mean it" or "They were hurting so the anger came out at an obvious target: *me*." This well may be true. However, *continuing* to allow ourselves to be put in such a position is self-destructive.

Letting persons know in a clear but kind way that they are behaving poorly is one way to deal with it. In some cases, limiting contact with the person is another. Certainly, although we must honestly admit that *none* of us are angels, we need to recognize as well that neither are we the devil! And so, taking what is said to us that is very negative to heart in a way that is upsetting and a form of mini-trauma is dysfunctional and makes no sense, no matter what the other person says is true about us.

No one benefits in such instances—including the other people in our lives who count on us for support and can't receive it if we are psychologically limping because we have overly embraced hurtful comments and actions by one or a few persons.

Once I shared with a patient that she was giving me mixed messages. On the one hand, she was welcoming our contact by being on time for the sessions and working hard within them. On the other hand, the way she presented things was so off putting that she was pushing me away. In response, she asked, "Give me an example!" I related what she had just said to me and asked, "How would you feel if I said that to *you*?" Although she had an excuse, she at least heard what I said and could at some level feel the sad implications of continuing such behavior in her other relationships outside the session.

Caring is good. Retaliation for angry comments is not good. Yet, neither is simply positioning yourself under a box of verbal feces and either letting someone else pull the chain or doing it yourself by making excuses for the person while overly accusing yourself of wrongdoing. To prevent such unnecessary personal victimization at the hands of others or undue self-blame, we need to seek to be better at

- reflecting rather than immediately reacting to situations;
- recognizing and accepting that people often have expectations we can't meet and be OK with this;
- knowing what are healthy boundaries;
- not being unduly upset when we are misunderstood;
- preventing ourselves from being mistreated; and
- understanding that valuing others doesn't include not valuing or respecting ourselves because allowing people to treat us poorly doesn't help them realize their own unrealistic and unhealthy expectations of others—they may be hurting for some reason(s), but they need to change if their lives are to be as rewarding as possible going forward.

As Paolo Coehlo once quipped, there are times when we must "close some doors. Not because of pride, incapacity or arrogance, but simply because they no longer lead somewhere." Everyone who crosses our path in life has something to gain and something to teach us. Yet, not all of them are destined to do this for our whole journey on earth. Moreover, if someone pushes us away, it may be that they need the space to have someone else present to meet their needs in ways they value. We must honor that for their sake . . . and *ours*.

24

Images of Goodness

A while back, a colleague asked me, "Are you still traveling to speak on the prevention of *secondary* stress [the pressures experienced in reaching out to others] with helpers and healers around the world?" I told him that I was. In response, he gave me an impish smile and asked, "Well, how do you deal with your own *tertiary* stress in doing this then?" and I had to laugh.

Recently, this event came back to me. For personal reasons, as well as the anger and divisiveness that surround us in the government, society, and even in some religious institutions today, I felt a bit alone and sensed some sadness. This surprised me since I have a good life and am generally a fairly upbeat person.

When I experienced this, I leaned back mentally and reflected on what I was both feeling and thinking. I do this when I feel down so my sadness can become "*spiritual* sadness." By this, I mean that the gray periods in my life do not go to waste by me ignoring, running away, or making too much of them. Instead, I like to face them gently and clearly so that a lesson can arise to teach me about myself and how to live more compassionately rather than simply reacting in anger, hurt, or by simply withdrawing.

In this instance, what happened was surprising. Whereas usually a helpful thought comes to the fore, this time an image of a former student of mine who is a priest in Northern Ireland came to mind. I could see his smiling face, remember his kindness, and recall the tough times he had to face as a priest amidst the past "troubles" and current challenges in his country and ministry.

Almost instantly his image of goodness alleviated the fleeting sense of angst that I was experiencing. I knew that in undertaking my tender work with committed but discouraged physicians, nurses, educators, priests, ministers, police, relief workers, caregivers, and members of the military, I was not alone.

Images of goodness are wonderful reminders of the healing presence of goodness that will always be in the world even when all seems temporarily dark or gray. In difficult times, we need to recall the living community of "quiet saints" who aren't perfect and don't make a splash but can make a difference in life, *our* lives.

Know who those people are in your life and bring them to mind more often. Such images will help resurrect feelings of companionship and even inspire us to be better as friends to others as well.

25

"Little" Moments That Bring Tears of Joy to My Life . . . Even Now

> Sometimes you will never know the value of a moment until it becomes a memory.
>
> —Dr. Seuss

The "quiet moments with family" are the ones that strike me at this time in my life. I think of the Christmas tree I would lug home and decorate for my family. My parents would sit by it and smile.

I think of the times I would drive up to New Jersey to stay with my brother and sister-in-law. They would order pizza from Joe's around the corner, and while my brother, Ron, and I sat in the basement drinking cocktails, at the same time my sister-in-law, Noel, and my wife were chatting upstairs. Sometimes my nieces Deb and Chris would show up, and we would share stories and laughter while the dog stared at us. He was great at staring.

Before I enlisted in the Marine Corps, I remember coming down from Woodbourne, New York, where I worked at the Narcotic Addiction Control Commission. My mother-in-law knew I liked veal parmigiana, so she would have it ready, and then my wife-to-be and I would go to the White House Café with my brother-in-law and sister-in-law, Jack and Dotsy.

Many years later, I would spend time with my two granddaughters when they were small and everything was big to them. What fun. When you are little, everything is special . . . especially grandparents. I miss those times more than ever. I do.

None of these events were big deals in the eyes of the world. In retrospect, even though I have had a number of those so-called "big deals" in my life (someone once said, "You do know you are famous in certain circles?"), they were the more important moments. They were the big deals. They were the ones I remember now in this final phase of my life. I draw strength from them.

Naturally, there is sadness that these moments are gone. Yet, more than the sadness is the peace and joy that I was able to have such experiences. Not everyone is as lucky as I was and am. You know, maybe that is why I am able to do what I do and be there for professional helpers and healers in Syria, Haiti, Guatemala, Cambodia, as well as here in the United States. I have had a family's love, and when you have that, you can then walk with people who didn't have it . . . or have lost it all and sit quietly knowing that they have.

In the end, if we want to be persons who live a rich and meaningful life, it has to be a life for others. Yet, for that to happen, we have to have a good memory . . . a memory for those "little" moments when love was there for us in life. Such memories and stock-taking are certainly an important part of the quiet moments when you are mentoring yourself.

Not just the present is important. We also need to remember those past experiences of love in our lives . . . it was there in some way, maybe many ways. It is our heritage and grounding for now and the future. Moreover, it can bring tears of joy to our lives even now, and that's important if we wish to gain, maintain, or regain a healthy perspective in difficult times.

26

An Unexpected Harvard Experience . . . Why Don't You Try It as Well?

One of the most important encounters I had and realizations I received in my own life was in an encounter at Harvard University with the psychologist and spiritual writer, Henri Nouwen. To many people—including some of his friends—Henri often seemed to be a complex, even contradictory person. Yet, underneath all of this conflicting surface energy I believe was a simple, beautiful man who loved his priesthood, truly cared for others, and just wanted to do the right thing with his life.

His allure for me and so many others who met him personally, on the lecture circuit, and through his books was his uncanny ability to take his own specific experiences, feelings, and reflections and then write or speak about them in a way that touched a deep common chord. Most people who read Henri find at least one book that they believe was written *just for them*.

My feeling about Henri's writings parallels that of singer Dave Alvin's about the folk composer Kate Wolfe. Although Alvin had never met her, he was deeply moved by her song "These Times We're Living In." He wrote in the linear notes for the album, "I don't know much about Kate Wolfe's life and loves, but in a few raw and tender lines, she sure knew a lot about mine."

Henri was able to share feelings that we all experience but seem to elude expression for us. We can't seem to find the right words to capture them. Whereas, he is able to name and describe what we are feeling often enough for us to take his writing, stand on it, and make more sense of what we are about through it, so we can then go spiritually and psychologically where we have to journey in our own lives. That's what I often feel when I read Henri's writings, especially the early works.

Furthermore, that we often don't know where to go next seems more acceptable after reading about Henri's own personal confusion and discernments. At a certain level, our struggles don't seem much different than his. When he gets lost, complains, or is petty, we nod and think: "Been there. Done that." (Or, more accurately, "Am *still* there, doing that!") Then, as we move through one of his books, as he gains greater clarity, we seem to do so as well. It's a wonderful supportive feeling when his journey toward discernment becomes ours. His spiritual friendship with us through his writing frees us.

My meeting with him came at a turning point in my own life. It is one I have shared in my lectures for more than 35 years because the positive reactions I receive from those present continue to encourage me to do so. By the expression on people's faces, I can see that I have struck a chord. It is almost as if they mentally lean back and say, "To approach myself in this way is so simple to try. Why don't I take out some time to reflect upon this and see what it would mean in my case?"

What happened was that I was speaking to him about a theme for a new book I was writing that I had planned to title *Relationships: Nurturing the Gift of Availability.* His response was almost immediate: "For most of us, availability is not simply a gift. It is a problem!" He then searched himself to find a theme or concept that would explain how we could approach the issue of availability so it could remain a gift we give to others but also were prudent in how this gift could be both nurtured and shared. Finally, after we had spoken about other things for a while, his face suddenly lit up and he said, "I have it!" The theme we are looking for is: *Pruning!* When you prune something, it doesn't blossom less, it blossoms more deeply."

For me, that meant initially pruning my availability to others. I learned that in trying to be all things to all people, the quality of my presence would be lost, plus I would be involved in pursuits that had nothing to do with me. They should be carried on by others, including possibly the person asking me for help. And so, I developed an approach. If someone asked me to do something that I definitely wanted to and thought I should do, I said, "Yes, of course." If it were something totally beyond my abilities, I would simply decline. However, in most instances, it fell in the middle and I was unsure. And so, I would tell the person,

> I can see why you are asking me to do this. It certainly is within my area and interests me, and I don't want to hold you up on my response. After I get back to the office, I will look at my schedule and other activities, check with those with whom I work and will get back to you *first* thing tomorrow *if I can do it.*

In this way, I would not be getting into another round of discussions as to why I should or "must" do it according to the person inviting me.

However, an unusual thing happened to me after I returned home. I thought, What if I applied this same principle to my own personality? And so, since I am a quite passionate person, I decided to use "gentleness" as a way to prune my passion so I could at least try to be a more gentle passionate person. Following this, many years later, I felt called to take the next and probably final step with respect to embracing and sharing my identity more fully. I focused more on the process of pruning (gentleness) than on the core identity I believed I had (being passionate).

As a result, although most people will recognize me forever as a person of great energy and passion, I decided to bring the spirit of gentleness front and center. I wanted to ask myself as I met each day, "How am I being gentle? Is this humor gentle or hurtful? How can my gentleness give people the space to be more themselves?"

Now, for each person, their core identity and pruning word will be different. For some, their core identity may be as a person who is a great listener. So, for them, the pruning might be to be a more assertive listener so they speak up more often in order to share what they have heard and what they believe. Trying what I call now "The Harvard Experience" will be different for each of us but, as you can tell from this story, I believe an essential approach to living more fully for all of us is:

> to prune our personality so it is experienced and shared more richly—especially during uncertain and difficult times for us and those around us.

I think the results might surprise you . . . I know they surprised me.

27

One of the Most Serious Blocks to Mentoring Yourself

> It isn't that they can't see the solution, it's that they can't see the problem.
>
> —G. K. Chesterton

A few years ago, I was visiting a colleague after he had moved to a new townhouse community. He became tired of working on his yard and was getting up in years and so wanted less outside maintenance as well. When I asked him about the move, he responded enthusiastically:

> "Really great neighborhood. I like the layout of both the interior of my house and the community. Backing up to the woods is absolutely perfect."
>
> "How about the people? What are they like?" I asked.
>
> "Oh, for the most part they are terrific. There are a few narcissistic types but all in all I like them—including the narcissists, although they can be pests at times."
>
> "How can you tell they are narcissists and how are they annoying?"
>
> "Well I have administered the 'recycling test.'"

I knew he loved intriguing me with these kinds of statements, so I played along:

> "The recycling test?"
>
> "Yes, if on a windy day recycling is blown around, I watch and listen to their reactions to it. If they are walking along and pick up the stray box or plastic bottle and put it in a nearby bin, they are not narcissistic. If they see other people's recycling blowing around, do nothing, and blame the person for not packing it correctly while, on the other hand, blaming 'the wind' when it is *their* recycling tossed about, they get the diagnosis of narcissist."

Hearing this I had to laugh because I knew he was exaggerating things to entertain me. However, hearing it reminded me of how psychologically blind narcissistic individuals can be, so in self-mentoring, our narcissistic tendencies need to be carefully examined. Also, in the extreme, very narcissistic people can do great harm but remain hidden.

For instance, when leaders in the areas of corporate life, religion, politics, entertainment, and sports appear clinically depressed or unduly anxious, others within their organization become naturally concerned. However, paradoxically, such individuals, when receiving treatment (psychotherapy and/or medication), can be the most helpful and creative leaders because of their own heightened sensitivity to the plight of human existence. Not so with narcissistic personality disorder (NPD).

The problem with NPD is that it is often confused with persons simply having a slightly inflated ego, being somewhat "full of themselves," or demonstrating the "normal" traits of an assertive executive. Instead, the symptoms and signs of NPD, although varying in severity and presence, include

- the need for extreme, unwavering admiration;
- constant exaggeration or fabrication of achievements, personal gifts, talents, importance, and influence;
- monopolization of attention and conversations;
- a tendency to be sarcastic, belittling, and condescending to others;
- an absence of humility or self-reflective behavior that would lead to owning their own role in a problem in order to be motivated to change;
- preoccupation with thoughts and dreams about personal attractiveness, power, and success;
- a willingness to take advantage of others;

- an expectation of complete loyalty and compliance without feeling the need to return the favor;
- an inability to be aware of, and respect, the feelings, needs, or achievements of others; and
- lack of awareness of their own arrogant, conceited, pretentious, and boastful manner.

What makes this mental disorder even worse is that it is difficult to help persons with NPD become aware of or deal with it. Even if, for some reason, they come for treatment, they usually react very negatively and resistantly to anything they perceive as criticism. The result is that often they become

- dismissive of any suggestion of wrongdoing on their part—it's someone *else* who is at fault;
- explosive in response to any feedback, no matter how factual, that interferes with their own self-image;
- emotionally upset if they can't get their view wholly embraced by others;
- difficult to deal with because of an inability to regulate their speech or control their anger; and
- easily and immediately offended when they believe they are not appreciated enough for what they perceive they have done for someone else.

Given these symptoms, signs, and the failure to accept feedback that would lead to improvement of NPD, the question that often arises is: Why would people put them in a position of power or influence in the first place?

There are a number of reasons for this. One is that persons with NPD often have no censor of what they say. And so, they may appear to others as refreshingly candid and honest. This is very attractive at a time when there are so many people whose style is contrived or politically correct. Another attraction is that in the short term, persons with NPD may appear charming until they are challenged or disagreed with. Finally, persons with NPD are very sensitive to their audience's fears and self-interest and are able to appeal to them based on these factors.

If it is true that the unreflective life is not worth living, then when you have someone with NPD leading an organization, life can be made very difficult—and even dangerous—for those the person has power over. The actions and policies of persons with NPD are taken for only one thing: self-preservation of the false image of their own exaggerated sense of self-importance. Persons around them can exacerbate this problem. Because of *their own* insecurities, shortcomings, or desire for power and influence, others may enable such unhealthy narcissistic behavior, thus making the situation worse . . . *much* worse.

And so, "being small" (which is the opposite of NPD) allows us not to think of ourselves as a "special person" but as one gifted with uniqueness. In viewing ourselves this way, self-mentoring is conducted with the joy and peace that we don't need to measure up. Instead, we are called to "simply" be ourselves. That is accurate and grand enough.

Therapists hopefully learn to do this rather than wrap themselves in the mantle of "doctor" when they treat people. The advantage is that when those who are fearful and upset come in to see therapists and take a "psychological swing" at them, the therapists' egos will be too small for them to be hit. When this happens, rather than reacting, therapists can reflect with patients who are in distress as to why they were expressing so much anger at them. This can then lead to understanding rather than a repeat of the very problems the patients had in the world because of their negative behavior.

This same hope that therapists have for themselves is one all of us should have for ourselves. This is so we can be "small enough" to benefit from feedback from others; so we are not a poser in how we present ourselves; and in order to benefit more deeply from our own quiet, self-mentoring periods during the day.

The following very, *very* basic reflection of mine shares this hope quite succinctly. Maybe it will stir up some thinking on your part.

Being Small

I like being small.
It is fun for me.

I'm able to fit into places
others can't be.

Horses approach
rather than stay away.

Children smile
when I come their way.

Being invisible works
with large egos, as well.

Not only for me
but also for them.

Because when I share
they don't know it's a gift.

So freely enjoy
because there's no debt.

The funny thing is
that "large people" can follow

when they are authentic
and "simply ordinary" as well.

Yes, I like being small.
It is fun for me.

I wonder what would happen
if that's what all of us would be?

28

Honoring "Alone Time"

> I need to take a sacred pause, as if I were a sun warmed rock in the center of a rushing river.
>
> —Dawna Markova
> Founder and CEO Emerita
> Professional Thinking Partners

> The poet [Rilke] watched [sculptor] Rodin grow silent and closed off while he listened to music, "as before a great storm."
>
> —Rachel Corbett
> Author, *You Must Change Your Life*

Two road signs point to the need for, and challenge of, alone time. One was alongside the road entering a small but expanding Southern town that advised

> Dear people who just moved here,
> we don't honk the second the light turns green.
> This is the South.
> Simmer down.

The other sign I remember seeing as I approached a road construction project leading into Washington, DC, had written on it the warning,

> Prepare to be frustrated.

Alone time, which is time spent in silence and solitude or reflectively even while in a group, sometimes can be frustrating if we are used to always being on the move. Yet, it helps us to simmer down while challenging us to change in ways that are countercultural in today's noisy, constantly electronically linked society. To appreciate the need and be willing to meet the countercultural experience of silence, solitude, and reflection, we must first recognize that alone time is not idleness or a waste of precious moments in life.

Instead, if taken properly, it can add to our resilience by providing the space to repair and learn from the psychological challenges and damage of the day's encounters—although the benefits may at first blush seem to be elusive! In the words of the Buddha, when asked what he had gained from meditation (a concentrated version of alone time), he replied,

> *Nothing*! However, let me tell you what I have lost: Anger, anxiety, depression, insecurity, fear of old age and death.

A little time by yourself in the morning can lead to greater inner freedom during the day. Becoming attuned to the "crumbs of alone time" during the remainder of the day can reap the rewards of newly felt freedom through moments of mindfulness. In addition, when solitude is honored in the right way and nourished by silence, it can make interactions with others richer and more rewarding.

As Sara Maitland notes in a reflection on time alone contained in *A Book of Silence*, "Suddenly the amount of time in the day expanded, and there was more freedom and space and choice." She saw embracing such space as "a gentle movement towards a new way of living that gave [her] an increasing deep satisfaction."

Yet, somehow people who take time alone feel they are doing something countercultural. Even Maitland, in experiencing a substantial period by herself, wrote that she felt "foxy," that she'd "slipped [her] leash and got away."

Still, those who bring silence and solitude into the daily rhythm of their lives seem clearer and more at peace than they might be if they hadn't. Quiet time alone can become a gentle teacher of clarity and an experience of life not possible while adrift in a noisy world or within a cocoon of unexamined and unaddressed thoughts.

Silence and solitude are gentle friends who don't lie to us about ourselves. Instead, they slowly help us become familiar with life so we can flow better with it *as it is.* Without such periods, the risk is that we will be led by the familiar but untested thoughts and habits. We will also be driven to act by what we see in the eyes of others, and following a script from values that may not even be our own. Is that a meaningful life? Moreover, how resilient can we be relying so much on others' views of us.

However, while beneficial, traveling through the geography of silence and solitude takes courage, commitment, understanding, and humility. Although freeing, renewing, and clarifying (three seeds of resilience), to enter this inner territory is a lesson in vulnerability. If silence and solitude are true, they cannot be bribed. Otherwise, we are simply alone with our own ego, going round in circles, rather than deeper into ourselves and life. If we are transparent in our quiet moments, however, they will let us know where we are spiritually and psychologically located. This may surprise and be different than what others and even maybe what we have told ourselves up to this point. How intriguing is that?

29

Avoid the Three Blind Alleys

During a long snowstorm, hurricane, or a pandemic, people usually spend more time indoors. Even if they normally put on music or the television to break or avoid silent periods, somehow they have a chance to spend real extended time with themselves, with who they are.

In such prolonged times of being alone in silence and solitude, or even in actual mindfulness meditation, some people find that their selves are "softened." When this happens, they are often more gentle and clear about themselves and forgiving of others. Yet, this is not a given. Others see periods of "alone time" (time in silence and solitude or reflection even when in a group) as a space that often becomes filled with negative feelings. These include disappointment and anger at others, a heightened awareness of personal mistakes made in the past, or discouragement with the current state of affairs.

And so, to lessen the chance that alone time will be negative, but instead offer new opportunity for enjoying "the now" and being open to new wisdom in order to be better able to experience life in generative ways, there are three blind alleys to be aware of and avoid. This will allow an appreciation of an "open psychological road" to enjoy exploring life and one's changing presence in it.

The first blind alley is the most dangerous because it involves the most primitive psychological defense and will close off any avenue for true spiritual seekers. It is the *arrogance* that results from *projection*—always looking outward for the cause of any problems. In such an instance, it is never or rarely "our fault." Projecting the blame onto others for what we don't like in life may seem to be a nice way of avoiding the growing edges in ourselves. However, when we give away all the blame, we also give away most of the power to change things for the better.

The second blind alley is *ignorance*. This ignorance arises not when we blame others but when we continually condemn ourselves. Some people erroneously think such self-debasement is a way to humility, but it is far from that. Actually, behavior that we wince at will eventually turn into behavior that we wink at because it is impossible to constantly berate ourselves for our mistakes in the past and present. It will only lead to guilt that will pull us into the past and leave us there. This is much different than looking clearly, but kindly, at our mistakes. In doing this, we don't gloss over our faults but instead—with a true sense of remorse—pick ourselves back up, don't fall prey to desperation, and seek to move ahead with the added knowledge we now have gained about ourselves. This is not done with the expectation that we will immediately be able to change. The attitude instead reflects the humility that comes from knowing we have faults and are seeking to live with them in a better way by dusting off our talents and gifts.

The third blind alley is *discouragement*. This occurs when we don't see the changes we want in others, ourselves, or the world at large. Life goes through phases, as does our family and society. The question is how we will flow rather than drift or fight with such changes.

I remember speaking with one woman who was so upset. When I asked her what she believed was the source of her unease, she replied that her 50-year-old daughter was still behaving the same way she did as a youngster. I smiled at her, winked, and said, "And so, your response is that for 50 years you have been upset that she is not behaving as the woman you would have her be?"

This upset person was in such contrast with another woman, a Catholic missionary, I met during my travels who always seemed unperturbed despite the challenging work she undertook as a relief worker for a missionary group. When I asked this person if she could account for her sense of inner peace even in the midst of great poverty, in response she first simply smiled. Then after thinking about what I had asked for a few seconds, she said, "I do what I can and let others and God take care of the residue. This helps me not become discouraged when I face poverty or try to improve myself."

My thinking is that this person and others like her whom I have met—often in the midst of situations that would be overwhelming for many of us—have an ability to draw from their quiet time. Even in small doses, such time is like a fresh pool of perspective within themselves that they can relish when they are alone and quiet.

How can they do this? Well, instead of seeking to blame others, pick on themselves, or psychologically drown themselves in discouragement, they wrap themselves in a spirit of *intrigue*. They are as intrigued about their failures as they are about their successes and the gifts they have. They are intrigued about others rather than seeking to blame or fashion them to be less than themselves. They are also intrigued about the world around them and where their life will lead—even at its end.

A woman like this who was dying was asked by her son if she was afraid of what came next. She responded, "Not really. Just curious." This attitude didn't simply dawn on her at the end of life. It obviously filled her in each present moment so she could be intrigued and enjoy her life all through the years. During self-mentoring, we can ask, how might I be more like this enlightened woman? It is possible, you know.

30

Kindness Wears Many Different Types of Clothes

> Resolve to be tender with the young,
> compassionate with the aged,
> sympathetic with the striving,
> and tolerant with the weak and wrong.
> Sometime in your life,
> you will have been all of these.
>
> —Gautama Buddha

> When I give food to the poor,
> they call me a saint.
> When I ask why the poor have no food,
> they call me a Communist.
>
> —Dom Helder Camara

Kindness is a beautiful virtue that is admired when it spontaneously shows itself. This is especially when children are hurting. CNN reported the story of a little girl who could not go out in public because of a weakened immune system due to the cancer treatment she began receiving 2 days after her third birthday.

One of the joys up to that point for her was having Sunday lunch almost every week at J. Wilson's Restaurant. It was a family event before her treatments began but needed to stop because she couldn't be near other people.

When she would see the restaurant from the highway, she would ask her parents if she could go in. Her father was brokenhearted that he had to tell her no.

The manager of the restaurant, Paula Breaux, heard about the girl's story from a friend of the family. In response, she said, "We didn't have to think twice about it." She went ahead and arranged for the restaurant to be opened at a special early hour for the little girl and her family, and she even decorated the place in the girl's favorite color—pink—and made biscuits, which were her favorite food. Finally, when the little girl's mother went to pay the bill, she was told it was already taken care of. Her response to this was, "I can't explain how much this means to me, her dad and her sister."

Stories such as this warm our hearts. It certainly did mine. I read it at a time when I was tired and felt empty. It brought tears to my eyes that surprised and informed me that I needed to become more aware of my own self-care. However, it also reminded me that we so often hear about bullying, name-calling, cheating, and other failures to love but not so often about those who model loving behavior. It is important for us to remember those stories too, even about those who are afar—who at this very moment are showing selfless kindness toward others.

Yet, although kindness is usually fairly straightforward, it is at times often more complex than it may seem on the surface. Also, its expression may be more challenging than simply "being nice" or silent in the face of rejection, anger, or belittling comments.

Once, when I was teaching at a particular institution of higher learning, I met one of the administrators in the hallway. Much to my surprise, she made a sarcastic comment that caught me off guard. Later that day, I mentioned it to another psychologist. He asked in return, "Well, what did you say to her after she said that?" I smiled and said, "Nothing," with an expression on my face that was meant to convey "Wasn't I good?" The expression didn't last long because he responded, "Well, then, you didn't help her very much to recognize her own behavior for what it was, did you? You should have calmly asked her, 'Are you angry at me or someone else because you are coming across in an angry fashion?'"

Kindness wears many different types of clothes. It may be, as was just illustrated, giving persons a chance (whether they take it or not) to see how they are coming across that is pushing people away. Kindness also has us ask what is our unique role in expressing it. For example, it may be moving from an immediate act of kindness to a more systemic one, as in the case of Desmond Tutu, who once commented, "We need to stop just pulling people out of the river. We need to go upstream and find out why they're falling in."

A lack of kindness is also excused as "necessary" at times. Yet, we need to be careful when we equate being strong or resilient with a lack of gentle care for others. President Franklin Delano Roosevelt appreciated this in noting "human kindness has never weakened the stamina or softened the fiber of a free people. A nation does not have to be cruel to be tough." However, despite those words, when fear comes into play, it is easy to be cruel even if we know better. The fact that Roosevelt locked up Japanese Americans without due process or with consideration only of their country of origin graphically and sadly evidences this.

Similarly, there have been a number of reports recently about the stress of the job and bullying in the National Health Services in the United Kingdom. This echoes the reports of bullying of some nurses by other nurses in the United States health care system. It is a puzzle to me why people who contribute to reducing pain and stress in others have a remarkable capacity to cause stress for each other. Michael Lapsley, in his book *Redeeming the Past: My Journey from Freedom Fighter to Healer*, also talks about it in his description of the group he belonged to in Cape Town after the end of apartheid that worked to help victims of the apartheid years. He wrote, "It was remarkable that though we were a trauma centre we continued to inflict trauma on each other."

And so, we are not protected from secondary stress even if we work for one of the finest relief organizations of its type in the world. And, I am speaking not only about those who solely are involved in the intense fieldwork of caring organizations but also about the headquarters staff. As a matter of fact, they may even be in *more* danger because of their wonderful organizational mission.

The journal *The Economist*, published an article titled "Charity Begins at Work" (June 8, 2019) that explains this clearly. Here is what a section of the article noted (p. 65):

> The report was devastating. The working environment at the organization was described as "toxic." There was widespread bullying of staff and a bunker mentality among senior

> management; 39% of employees developed mental or physical health issues as a result of their work. An investment bank or a technology firm in Silicon Valley? No. This was Amnesty International, a human-rights charity. Five managers have just left the organization following the report's findings. . . .
>
> The report . . . makes clear that many employees regarded their job as a "vocation or life cause" that provided them with "a compelling sense of purpose and meaning." But that commitment proved to be a double-edged sword.
>
> First, in the eyes of workers, managers believed the importance of the NGO's work was so great that they did not need to listen to staff concerns. Employees, the higher-ups seemed to conclude, "should be grateful for being able to work at Amnesty." Secondly, workers found it difficult to set healthy boundaries on their hours (or on their tolerance of a toxic climate) owing to a deeply held belief in the mission. . . .
>
> Concerns came to a head when . . . a long-time employee committed suicide blaming work pressures . . . [eventually leading to] the commissioning of a report.

The article then ends making the following point: "The bosses at Amnesty International may have listened to the political dissidents whose causes they were championing. But they clearly weren't listening to their staff."

Kindness to others has a simple goal: to demonstrate to others that they matter—especially if the person works or lives with us and is easy to take for granted. There is also a danger that we may take the hurt we have experienced from those we have tried to help and project it onto those to whom we feel safe venting our anger.

Kindness is also often misunderstood for passivity. Yet it is the moral engine that turns on our sense of righteousness when we see those suffering in our country and want to help them while others are primarily concerned whether they came here illegally before they reach out.

Romanian-born American writer, professor, political activist, Nobel Laureate, and Holocaust survivor, Elie Wiesel, once proclaimed, "I swore never to be silent whenever and wherever human beings endure suffering and humiliation. We must always take sides. Neutrality helps the oppressor, never the victim. Silence encourages the tormentor, never the tormented."

Finally, kindness also requires us to look further to see what is underlying a person's pain and the suffering they may have added to it. In some cases, it is not our job to intervene, but even if that is the case, we should at least back off in a way that doesn't add more hurt to the person who is lost. In this way, there is space for someone else to enter the scene who can be more helpful. We don't need to force our type of support on others when it is not helping the situation.

A similar note can be said of our *receiving* kindness. When we meet people—even those we may barely know—if we see they seem to appreciate the heaviness we are experiencing, the reticence in our interaction, and a mute rather than bright voice, these are the persons to welcome into our day. Such moments are essential if we are to regain resiliency.

One of the overarching goals of mentoring yourself is to appreciate the different nuances of kindness, in different situations, with different people, experiencing different stresses. Also, as was previously emphasized, such an honoring of different facets and demonstrations of kindness must also include the multifaceted components of *self*-kindness.

31

A Very Dangerous Fear

Soon after I finished my doctoral studies in psychology at Hahnemann Medical College and Hospital in Philadelphia, I joined a faculty in Pennsylvania with quite wonderful colleagues. They really cared about their students and the clinical work they were guiding them to do. One of them stood out for me as especially talented. And so, I was both surprised and empathic to her situation when she said she was worried about qualifying for promotion.

"What do you have to worry about?" I asked in a puzzled voice. She replied, "I am fine with respect to service to the department and university. Also, I have excellent student evaluations of my teaching. The problem is that other than a few articles, I have not published much."

Since I had already written a number of books, I asked her, "Well, what about writing a book?" She looked at me as if I was crazy, so I said,

> Let me break it down for you:
>
> Come up with a common clinical problem that you are very familiar with.
>
> Seek to approach it in a unique way given your particular understanding of how to deal with it.
>
> Break your idea into 10 points which will be your chapter headings.

> For each of the points, develop several illustrations, usual pitfalls, and how to avoid them.
>
> And, finally, put together a manuscript proposal based on the outline I will give to you that I have found pretty helpful in the past.

She laughed and said, "You make it sound so simple!" "It is," I replied. "Not easy—but certainly straightforward, doable, and, yes, *simple*."

Following that, I guided her through the process of preparing her submission, finding the right publishers that released a title such as hers, and cheered her on. After that, I forgot about it until finally one day it dawned on me she hadn't mentioned anything about it for about a month, so I asked her, "Did you ever get any positive response to your manuscript proposal?" She looked at me, a little surprised, and said in a quite lively manner, "Oh, *yes*. I received an offer and accepted it."

Now, *I* was puzzled. "Well, why didn't you tell me?" To which she responded candidly in a way I would probably have never shared even if I felt that way, "Oh, I thought if I told you it worked out, you would feel I was indebted to you for the help you gave me." I was speechless. Truly. Verbally I said nothing, although I am sure my face gave away my sense of incredulity. We never spoke about it again.

A fear of indebtedness is more dangerous than people realize. First of all, if the source of it is not understood and confronted, the person will go through life with a sense of entitlement, expectations for graciousness offered, and an inability to appreciate the many gifts that come with life. The sense will be that "I earned it all" when in fact, *no one* earns it all no matter how hard they may work.

What is also a problem for those who fear being grateful is that they will miss so much that is already in their lives. Grateful people both see and enjoy more than those who have a sense of entitlement and, under the guise of social justice, are constantly looking for where they have been cheated, ignored, or let down.

One of the key aspects of self-mentoring is to continually use the lens of gratitude for what is around us that we might be missing. An end-of-the-day reflection with appreciation as a guide to reviewing the interactions one has had and situations one has been in also is a good idea. This isn't meant to gloss over what has been painful or ignore any rejections felt. Instead, it serves as a balance to the negative so one doesn't see life in a single dimension of darkness. Also, it helps us see that even in tough times, there are gifts that arise that we would have missed if we hadn't been deprived or challenged at that time. When life gets tough, our eyes of gratefulness need to be even sharper. The positive results in such instances may be quite surprising.

Practically everyone, including the past colleague of mine just mentioned, would probably respond affirmatively if asked, "Are you a grateful person?" Yet, in my case as well as most people I know (there are a few amazing exceptions whom I have encountered), we should really respond, "I'd like to feel I am but I know I am missing so much more in my life that is already there but I lack the appreciative eyes to see."

Through intentionally attending to the theme of gratitude when mentoring ourselves, any unconscious tendency to take things for granted, or miss the real value of it, will lessen. And when this happens, an increase in a tendency to use grateful eyes more often will arise. The results can be amazing.

32

Eat the Food . . . Not the Menu!

As I mentioned at the beginning of the book, someone I know does group work with older clients whose main challenge is being frozen by having a negative attitude toward life. He describes them as persons "waiting patiently for the past to change."

His words stuck with me and seemed to resonate with those of the training analyst supervising me when I studied more than 40 years ago at Hahnemann Medical College and Hospital. I had been presenting to him a case of a woman who seemed caught in the past and having difficulty moving forward in life. I sympathized with her since she was a truly good person who had some terrible luck but didn't know what to do going forward. The verbal interventions I made seemed to fall on deaf ears.

After listening to me for a while, the training analyst smiled and said,

> Doctor, you seem to have met serious resistance to change. If you take on such a psychological resistance directly, you will lose. On the other hand, possibly by offering her an image to reflect upon may be of help in getting around her resistance. Explain to her that when we break an egg on a hot pan, the heat has an impact on the albumin in the clear part of the egg and changes it to white. No matter what we try to do to that egg after that will change the white part back to clear. Also, if we take a rose and crumble it, we can take the petals and make

a lovely collage out of them . . . but, we will never be able to reassemble the rose to what it was. The change is permanent, no matter how much and how long we may wish it to be different.

In addition, she needs to recognize that after the loss of life as she knew it, she may also be tempted to look to find out why this happened to her. However, there often is no "why" and as long as time is spent on that, moving forward is not possible. How we move forward is the way to go and maybe if she can recall the images I just shared, it will help her cognitions move from focusing on "the why" and "the past" to moving ahead. She may then have the impetus to make the changes necessary to enjoy herself now and going forward. She sounds like "a good soul" who deserves to get as much out of life as she can. Maybe the images will help her let go and move on.

The same can be said with respect to a crisis such as the coronavirus. Some people are spending a good deal of time seeking to blame those who they believe started it all. And so, you hear, "It's the Chinese!" No, it is not. No matter how some of us would like to project the blame onto some group as a way to relieve us of our own responsibility, the situation is usually far more complex.

Others erroneously focus on the past and ask, When will we return to "normal"? Naturally, we want this to be framed in a way that sounds sensible, so we call it "the new normal." Yet, wishing that this will be possible as a way to experience the immediate "benefit" of denial—avoiding something unpleasant—still won't help us make the most of the present time we are in and help us be creative in future planning. Fantasizing about a complete return to pre-crisis living is just like the persons who sit around waiting for the past to change. It won't happen. Doing it as a way of coping with the unknown is, at some level, understandable. However, a steady diet of it, in the end, is not helpful.

Making the most of the present new way of living and seeking to prepare as much as possible for the options going forward may not be as much fun as nostalgia or waiting for "the new normal." But, when we make the most out of reality rather than steeping ourselves in fantasy, our lives improve. Once in a while, mentally "running away" is OK, natural, and may be helpful. But having a full diet of fantasy is like trying to live on eating a fancy menu rather than making the most of the modest but nurturing food on the plate in front of us.

Once again, the choice is up to us. Hopefully, with some quiet reflection and the influence of psychologically healthy friends and family members, we can do this—not in the spirit of resignation but with a sense of gratitude for all that was practically invisible in our daily routine but is available now in simple, nourishing ways because a crisis in life has revealed it all to us for our benefit and enjoyment. Tragedy, trauma, darkness, ongoing stress, and, yes, even a pandemic can sometimes do that . . . *if* we have the psychological and spiritual "eyes" to see.

33

Being Friendly with Yourself

Failure and Self-Forgiveness

> And God said, "Love your enemy" and I obeyed him and loved myself.
>
> —Khalil Gibran

In "resiliency psychology," my specialty for more than 35 years, one of the more recent areas of discussion and emphasis is referred to as "self-compassion." This may sound to some like narcissism or inordinate self-interest. However, healthy self-compassion has a proportionate impact on our ability to walk with family, friends, and co-workers in their darkness. This is so because one of the greatest gifts we can share with others is a sense of our own peace and inner strength . . . but we can't share what we don't have!

An essential cornerstone of such appropriate self-compassion is the ability to forgive ourselves when we fail. Compassionate persons fail a great deal. We probably don't like to talk about it, but it's true. As a group, we fail as much if not *more* than any other community concerned with helping others in need. This should not be surprising since with greater commitment there is a greater "opportunity" to miss at least some of the numerous goals we set for ourselves in life.

Yet, despite the fact that we court failure as a natural part of our idealism, many of us still punish ourselves mentally when we believe we have missed the mark—even if it was an almost impossible one. One of the most powerful ways of dealing with such a tendency in self-mentoring is to embrace a proper sense of forgiveness about what we have failed to do or accomplish in our work with others or in facing our own shortcomings.

To accomplish this, we must first recognize and avoid false forms of forgiveness. "Pseudo-forgiveness" often parades itself as a form of true self-awareness. However, by its "fruits" it is possible to discern in ourselves and others whether or not the sense of forgiveness is properly oriented. There are surely numerous forms of pseudo-forgiveness. The one that particularly concerns us here is the one that forgets our humanity, inordinately focuses on the shame of our failures, and leads to an unproductive confession based only on ventilation of our shortcomings.

Pseudo-forgiveness of self begins when, in trying to be compassionate, we forget that we can and *will* eventually fail. We forget that in trying to reach out to family, friends, co-workers, and even those in need who we do not know well, our own limits and needs must sometimes get in the way. When I was lecturing to a group of surgical residents on resilience, self-care, and maintaining a healthy perspective, I cautioned them with the reality that during their tenure as surgeons, they would probably kill some people—not necessarily because of malpractice but because of *mis*-practice. No one can operate on an "A" level 100% of the time no matter what their role.

Parents do get tired and yell at their children even when they recognize (possibly later) that this was not the best thing to do. Others are sometimes short-tempered or condescending to the poor or chronically ill in their midst when they are not fully rested, have eliminated the space for personal "alone time," or don't have enough balance in their schedule. At such times, it is easy to forget that we are not perfect. Yet, with the right outlook, we can learn from our failures rather than see them simply as proof that we shouldn't, or can't, be a compassionate presence to others in need.

When we are seeking to be faithful to what is good and lose our perspective with regard to failure, we may ignore the need for self-acceptance as a prelude to personal growth. In such cases, instead of forgiveness leading to an openness that will in turn translate into self-understanding, it leads to self-punishment or condemning others for their needs and situation. In such a case as this, we believe that we are seeking forgiveness by crucifying ourselves for our weakness. As we do this, the energy formerly reserved for knowledge gets destructively channeled off into changing the process of self-understanding into one of self-condemnation. Nothing positive is accomplished when this happens.

Ironically, this hurtful process of supposedly honest repentance *prevents* rather than enhances change and growth. The most obvious reason for this is that we are less apt to look at our behavior objectively if we are embarrassed or pained by reflection on it. If it causes us too much discomfort to look at something, psychologically we will avoid it through repression, suppression, denial, rationalization, and by general distortion of it.

So, how can we mine the fruits of personal failure when it occurs? First, I think our *attitude* is key. It will determine if we can weather the storms of failure and a sense of loss when our goals are not achieved. In her memoir, *Dakota*, author Kathleen Norris wrote that she was called to reflect on this when she had come across a handwritten note by her grandmother inserted in an old family Bible. On it was written, "Keep me friendly to myself; keep me gentle in disappointment."

The second element is *clarity*. Although we need to recognize the need to be kind so we don't cause narcissistic injury (hurt ourselves to the core of our personality), we also need to seek details about our failures, losses, and disappointments. If we are only gentle, we won't grow. If we only focus on our failures in a nonforgiving way, we will stunt our own growth. We need a balance of clarity and kindness in facing failure and forgiving ourselves for not being the person we wish to be in all situations.

The final element on the way to healthy self-forgiveness is to recognize that failure can teach us in much more powerful ways than success ever can. If we have the right balance of clarity and kindness, we will

- experience increased motivation and determination to face what we encounter as "darkness" or failure in ourselves;
- gain greater insight into who we are as persons because we will uncover our gifts, areas of vulnerability, and defenses;
- have less dependence on the recognition and approval of others;
- be in a better position to pick up more quickly the emotional cues that we are going to do something we will eventually regret so we can stop ourselves in time before we speak or act inappropriately;

- set the stage for the development of new skills and styles of interacting with others—especially in tough or chronically draining situations; and
- know we can't ride the waves of life's stresses alone and expect we can always achieve our goals and gain the perspective on our own to know how and when to forgive ourselves. As Reinhold Niebuhr, American ethicist, theologian, and commentator aptly notes, "Nothing we do, however virtuous, can be accomplished alone."

Finally, forgiveness of self also involves patience with ourselves so we can recognize that living a compassionate life involves tolerating discouragement and having the fortitude to continue despite the absence of immediate results.

In essence, when we truly understand the need for forgiveness of self when we fail, as we surely will at times, we will position ourselves to have a greater sense of inner peace that is independent of external success, comfort, and security. And, when we have such an attitude, think of what a gift we would be not only to ourselves but also to those we co-journey with as friend, family member, co-worker, or possibly in a professional role as helper or healer. Self-forgiveness is not a nicety. It is a necessity in today's anxious world in which people are so in need of compassion—including *self*-compassion.

34

Strengthening the Strong

As an author, sometimes I get so involved in writing even an email that I am oblivious to what is going on around me. However, when this occurs, fortunately I have an extra sense that allows me to feel when someone is near to me, waiting for an opportunity to say something.

On one of those occasions, as I was nearing the end of a delicate message to persons holding the power over others but who seemed to be missing a key element, I looked up from the keyboard and there was a close and talented colleague standing in the doorway. She didn't want to disturb me but obviously wanted to share something that was bothering her.

When I saw her face, I smiled. Though I desperately wanted to complete what I was doing in a manner that was precise, in a gentle voice, I simply said, "What?"

She responded, "I see you are busy so if you want I can come back but I would like to talk to you at some point."

Since she was so resilient and able to handle quite a bit, I was tempted to put her off. However, something in me realized that this would be a mistake. And so, I said, "No. Now would be good. Come in. Just give me a minute to save what I have been doing. Actually, I could use a break." (I'm not afraid to bend the truth a bit if need be.)

She sat down and related that she was worried about a medical issue. Since she had treated physicians for years and gone the extra mile for them, she felt free enough to ask for professional courtesy to be seen sooner than they initially could schedule her. In response, the receptionist who said she would check to see if this was possible never even called her back as she said she would.

Although she was put off by this, in and of itself, it was not enough to trouble her. However, around the same time a serious event occurred in her extended family in which she was treated quite poorly. When she stopped for a moment, I asked her, "Well, how did those in your immediate family respond to how you were treated?" She responded in a low voice, "No one even said anything. It was like it didn't happen. I think they were more concerned that I would make a fuss about it."

She went on to tell me that this really didn't surprise her since she was the strong and sane one in her genetic and even extended family but that it hit at a time when she could have used support.

In response, I smiled at her and said,

> Well, you are very resilient, flexible, and able to understand the reasons why people behave badly. That is your gift to those around you and the world. Yet, you must understand that in being this way, people often forget your needs and don't appreciate that even though you are strong, you could at times use a moment for support and gentle understanding yourself.

She got tearful at that moment, looked up at me, and expressed gratitude that amidst all I had on my plate, I had a moment for her. It seemed to make all the difference.

Everyone, including (maybe *especially*) those responsible for the care and support of others such as parents, ministers, therapists, nurses, educators, physicians, and caregivers, need support themselves at times. It is very important that we appreciate this when compassionate souls turn to us for support. And, if we are "the resilient one" in the family or a system, we also need to remember to turn to others who will understand that we need a kind word and a listening ear once in a while, too. Otherwise, we won't make it and that would be a shame.

And so, self-mentoring should surface a recognition of when and how we should seek healthy support. Otherwise, everything else we learn during this process will eventually fall by the wayside because we will become too emotionally exhausted to put the insights gained in mentoring ourselves into practice. Modeling strength for others includes feeling free to embrace and not hide our own vulnerability.

35

Mentally Moving in Uncertain Times

> The mind does not come to life until it meets something it cannot comprehend.
>
> —James P. Carse
> *Breakfast at the Victory*

Uncertain times often cause us to move out of ourselves. How we do this can determine whether we have retreated or are setting the stage to become deeper as persons. Since the process for both movements is so similar at times, it is difficult to know which we are doing.

When we have quiet moments amidst both chaos and boredom, one way we may cope is through fantasy. This retreat into fiction is understandable. Who wishes to live in a world in which control is impossible and normalcy is undependable? Fantasy allows us a respite from what is going on around us by going into a reverie. It is a mental island for us within the turbulent waters of emotion and a sense of being lost. In the moment, it is not a bad thing. It serves as a "psychological cortisone" to allay the negative impact we are feeling from such things as stress, a sense of alienation, loss, a crisis, or other ongoing unwanted outward force in life. However, just like the *continued* use of cortisone has an actual danger of masking a physical problem that needs to be dealt with before it gets worse, fantasy (our "mental cortisone") can prevent us from facing what we must in the world before our lives are derailed.

On the other hand, *dreaming*, which often looks like fantasy, is useful because it has two key differences:

- Just like fantasy, dreaming helps us break the bonds of our normal view of the world and ourselves. Yet, its sole purpose is not to escape our current situation. It is designed to open ourselves so we may entertain creative new options for living within our situation in the future.
- Unlike fantasy, dreaming doesn't give away all the power to mental images or other people. It retains it and acts upon it. Obviously, there is a real difference in watching a ball game in which our team wins and yelling "*We* did it!" and actually playing a ball game and our team winning it. There is a major difference between a person actually trying to make the world better and the "sideline critic" who risks nothing to improve the situation. The critic chooses the safe role of commentator, whereas the person in the fray seeking creative solutions is truly putting life on the line to help. (We could see this in the difference between health care workers seeking to treat pandemic victims and those who were out in the streets standing side by side protesting for the freedom to go out . . . and risk infecting others!)

Knowing the difference between fantasy and dreaming allows us to use fantasy judiciously so we can escape for a while. It also encourages us to dream dreams so we can discover new ways to make life better for ourselves and others. Dreaming is part of the process of mentoring yourself because it asks questions such as the following:

- What is the worst thing that could happen if I do this a different way or fail?
- Although I have led my life successfully in *a certain way* before, what is needed now that is different since life has changed and I want to make the most of this new world?

Ideally when we seek to mentor ourselves, we ask such questions because they are the type that those who mentored us in the past would have challenged us with when we were at an impasse. Remember that when we are at an impasse, it is not bad because it "freezes up" the left side of the brain, which is involved in problem solving and is normally of good service to us in daily life but is not helpful when we are stuck in an old way of thinking and behaving. Instead, when at an impasse, the right side of the brain, which deals with creativity, is given a chance to open up and offer us new possibilities.

If we don't shut down viewing such possibilities, then our world can expand. Otherwise, we will only shift back and forth between nostalgia and fantasy about a magical rescue. The more helpful alternative obviously is to embrace the new possibilities that an impasse offers when we are quiet, reflective, intrigued, and hopeful as a way of allowing a new dream to surface upon which to now act. If mentoring ourselves doesn't lead to a radically new vision and subsequent necessary change at times, it is too controlled and artificial. What good is that?

36

Seeing Through the Clouds

A number of years ago, I was at a conference in the Midwest of the United States. On one of the breaks, I took a walk with a longtime friend. En route, we met a scholar whom I really didn't know well. Both of us chatted about what we had written and done during the past years.

After we parted, my friend and I continued to walk and speak about the conference. When there was a lull in the conversation, he said to me, "Listening to the two of you talk back there sounded like the battle of two big egos." In response, I laughed but inside felt deeply hurt by his comment.

I know myself well enough that when I feel like that, the last thing I need to do is think about it immediately. The feelings of hurt would only result in me becoming defensive or in berating myself for being so egotistical.

Later on, when I felt more at peace and had some distance from the event and comment, I did reflect upon it. I know from experience in both offering and receiving guidance that the most valuable information from mentoring ourselves often results from surfacing both our positive and negative feelings. This would then lead me to look more clearly at the way I was thinking, perceiving, and understanding that led to such emotions.

From a distance, I now could see that it was true that I really love the work I do in helping others, mostly professionals, to increase their abilities at self-care, remaining resilient, and nurturing a healthy perspective in their work and life. I also love speaking about these topics and writing about them. All true.

However, what my friend was picking up was the poor motivation for the way I was sharing my efforts in these areas. It was as if I was trying to prove something to the other person . . . and maybe, *myself*!

When our ego gets involved, it clouds the scene. Instead of clarity about what is going on around and within us, our perceptions, and actions arising out of them, get distorted. When we get anxious, our ego prevents the flow of information. We move from being concerned about seeing clearly to seeing in a particular way that will help us feel better.

Two things that help us deal with this are honesty and a sense of humor. If we allow ourselves to calm down and let the rushing waters of our emotions and needs settle, we can see more deeply. And, if we can laugh at ourselves more often, we can poke a hole in the enlarged ego that is blocking our vision. Contemplative Thomas Merton once quipped that the false self doesn't like to be laughed at.

I think that is true. It is important to pick up when we are being exhibitionistic and tease ourselves as a way of maintaining or regaining a healthy sense of perspective about ourselves and the situations we are in. Unfortunately, on the way to taking crucial issues in life seriously, we sometimes take a detour and begin to take *ourselves* too seriously. This leads to a brittleness in our personality and interpersonal style. This is dangerous not only to us but also to those around us. If we are brittle because of egoism, when the psychological winds of stress, change, and discovery challenge us, like a tree that can't sway in the wind, we will break and the brokenness that leads to negativity will fall on those around us as well. We will become angry, harsh, sarcastic, belittling of others, and defensive in additional ways. And, this is even more dangerous when we are in the middle of an ongoing crisis when what is expected of us is transparency and vulnerability as a way of increasing the trust of those who count on us.

Self-reflection in such instances relies on realizing what our growing edges are and under what circumstances we will fall prey to narcissistic tendencies to attract attention to our achievements as a way of increasing our reputation with others. The irony is that such behavior usually has the opposite effect.

Whereas when we have an honest and balanced reputation with *ourselves*, then our self-esteem is not dependent on what others think of us. Instead, it allows us to smile at both our accomplishments and foibles because we realize that our happiness is not dependent on the former nor destroyed by the latter when we are friendly, balanced, and honest in our relationship with ourselves. Such a relationship with ourselves makes even more sense when we realize quite simply an obvious reality that is surprisingly often forgotten: *We are with ourselves more than anyone else.*

37

"The Future Is Not What It Used to Be"

> In the depths of winter, I finally learned that within me lay an invincible summer.
>
> —Albert Camus

The quote, "The future is not what it used to be" is attributed to many persons, including legendary New York Yankee baseball catcher Yogi Berra. It fits life today because the assumptions of most of us living now have been recently shattered by the initial and ongoing havoc caused by COVID-19.

When the pandemic took root, the sense of control and predictability we normally held became drastically disrupted. It also altered a sense of meaning-making for many of us. Work became not something we *go to* but something *we do*, even if the setting was our home. Religion became for many people not a practice in a building but, rather, an act of faith in one's heart and in connection virtually with others. Learning for our children didn't happen primarily on a campus. It occurred now on a computer—often in conjunction with other young people on theirs.

The other changes were caused by where and how widespread the impact was. Instead of the terror of rape, war, and other traumas happening *over there* to *other* people, it was a *pan*demic. In other words, by definition, it was visiting all of us—although our reactions to it were quite particular.

Some responded by following the guidelines of medical–nursing professionals and epidemiologists by doing what they could to take recommended, possibly unusual steps (i.e., wearing face masks) in order to protect themselves, keep others safe, and avoid overwhelming hospital critical care units.

Others demanded the "freedom" to risk infection by joining large rallies while unmasked. Ostensibly they did it to protest regulations that restricted them. Often, it was also really an unconscious reaction against having to confront and live very differently from the past. This is a natural reaction by some when encountering something life-threatening that the person cannot control or for which an ending cannot be predicted. However, when persons continue in this vein, they miss learning from the distress in ways that can offer rewards never encountered before.

And so, it is worth our while to embrace the following twofold approach to join with others who have not merely endured suffering but grown from crises in unimaginable wonderful ways:

- Face directly, rather than denying, seeking to go around, or glossing over unwanted aspects of a serious negative event (rape, torture, severe stress, loss, and possibly a pandemic for some).
- Be open to a radically different sense of meaning and living that would not have been possible had the horrible situation not occurred in the first place.

For such new depth and growth to be discovered, however, a conflict with previously held assumptions must be confronted. To recall the words of the "great philosopher" Yogi Berra again, we must truly accept that the future is not what it used to be. Finding out what it might be will take a true sense of openness as a way of learning greater compassion and discovering a new appreciation of life that we didn't fully acknowledge prior to the unwanted event. This is certainly better than rumination or fruitlessly seeking a return to the unreturnable past as a response.

It is "uncommon sense" that we need now. It is an honoring of a new portal we can humbly enter to gain new wisdom. Otherwise, we will forever remain standing on "the doorstep" of the next phase of our life complaining about the loss of past normalcy. The choice seems simple, but make no mistake about it: For many it is not easy . . . nor will they ever walk through the portal of change to meet life in a new, possibly undreamt of, way. They will insist that remaining on the doorstep of a new life, while protesting the loss of a past existence while new life that is possible passes them by, is the only natural or acceptable path to take.

When we take a few moments in silence and solitude to mentor ourselves, will it lead to the changes we need to meet and make? That is the question all of us must face.

38

A Strange Tension

A strange tension exists between honoring your own pain and welcoming a healthy perspective. The same can be said in our relationship with others when they are experiencing something unwanted.

When I would return from a trip to such places as Beirut, Haiti, Cambodia, or Guatemala or work with caregivers evacuated from Rwanda during the country's bloody genocide, my own sense of what was truly painful had a high bar. And so, when I returned to my clinical practice on Rittenhouse Square in Philadelphia, the troubles being experienced by my patients there seemed to pale by comparison.

As a way to make the transition between the two very different groups, I would often try to remain more silent when I returned. This would allow me some space to readjust to the new population with which I was dealing. What they were experiencing deserved my understanding as well.

What the more dramatic encounters abroad and with high-risk groups did for me, however, was to sensitize me more to the need for putting my own pain and that of those I normally dealt with in perspective. This was done by asking myself and others questions that would focus on the framework for evaluating our own sense of discomfort in order to see how we might be magnifying our own experience in comparison with the rest of the world.

The goal of this is not to make a person feel guilty for complaining. I wasn't seeking the response, "Oh, I know I have it good. I should be more grateful." Rather, the aim was to have people lean back and reflect on how they were interpreting the things and people who were causing discomfort in their lives.

In doing this, reframing the whole scene becomes possible. In this way, myself and others don't give away power to people and events that really don't deserve it. By widening our view of what should be classified as painful or discomforting, we gain a better perspective on life and the challenges we face. In addition, we may begin to have more energy and "emotional space" to deal with much more serious matters as well as to be grateful for the many things we do have and have had in life.

In approaching life this way, such a sense of gratefulness often has a paradoxical impact because it opens our eyes to what is already present in that we have underplayed. It also sets the stage for us to simplify our needs, rather than constantly expand them, so we can more deeply enjoy what is already within our reach: a cup of tea or coffee to leisurely enjoy, a book to read in the evening, music to listen to, a hot shower to relax our body, and an interesting sandwich to enjoy that was made with ingredients that maybe we had never before thought to combine.

A problem with this is that the world, and many around us, are threatened by such an attitude. The society in which we live is sometimes based on envy and consumption. In such cases, people want to convince us we need what we don't have and then sell us something that they tell us will make us feel satisfied and just maybe superior to others who don't have it.

Today, we are also often told that experiencing any discomfort, pain, or even suffering is unjust and intolerable, even though it is a normal part of life . . . just as death is. And so, a key question when we seek greater self-understanding that should confront us is: Do we rejoice when we are simply OK or only when we have something special before us or during the immediate moments after some pain or problem is relieved?

Naturally, it is difficult to rejoice always because we become grateful-tolerant to what and who are around us providing joy and satisfaction. And this is why taking out time each day for a few moments in silence and solitude while wrapped in gratitude for who we are and all we have is not to be taken lightly. Once again—and I can't re-emphasize it often enough—alone time is a *necessity*. Otherwise, the only time we will have perspective as to what is really important is when someone is sick or dies. What a shame to live life this way . . . yet many do. The question for us in self-mentoring is whether we want to join them or be more reflective so we don't lose perspective as often and are able to reframe life to get the most out of it—not simply for ourselves but also for those who see in us a model for living their journey.

39

You've Got an Attitude!

Facing resistances to understanding and then taking steps to change depend on the attitude we bring to a reflective period. Just as in the case of when someone approaches us formally or informally requesting mentoring, assessing our own attitude to lead the most meaningful life possible when mentoring ourselves is essential.

Positive signs of an attitude marked by openness and a sense of intrigue include the following:

- An ability to become disgusted with our own unhelpful attitudes and behavior
- A desire to unlearn and let go—even of those stances or beliefs that may have once been helpful but are no longer relevant
- Being receptive to a spirit of unlearning and open to absorbing new lessons
- A willingness to explore concerns about others to see our role in making the situation better or worse
- Being attentive to those emotions and thoughts that point to self-righteousness on our part and how they may be hidden by our claim to stand on principle
- Having a practice—even an informal one—of mindfulness meditation in which we are not only willing but desirous of taking out time to be in the now and be reflective

- Seeking to incorporate what we learn in self-mentoring into daily activities so the knowledge becomes reality in how we live and treat others
- Openness to new experiences and people—including ones different from our routine activities and interpersonal circle
- Fostering a sense of humor that allows us to both laugh at ourselves and take life lightly rather than make every event into something heavy or a game changer
- Being intrigued about what we perceive as negative in order to lessen our judgmental nature so we can be open and have a true sense of curiosity

In line with these signs, we also need to appreciate when we move away from such an attitude marked by "gentle clarity." We need to note those times when we respond instead with a sense of defensiveness, are argumentative, and focus on only the part of the issue where we look good or are comfortable examining or making excuses for not acting or complaining about others.

To "get around" such defensiveness, because you will never win taking on a resistance to change or habit directly (as in the case of mentoring others), the following are helpful points that can be made to ourselves in self-mentoring:

- Seek to see the examination of personal behavior, cognitions, and emotions with a sense of intrigue and neutrality—as if it were someone else reporting they are thinking or doing these things.
- Avoid criticizing or condemning ourselves as well as others; simply observe.
- Take notes on what we learn so it is possible to see patterns and avoid the defensive style of "forgetting" or minimizing ongoing mistakes.
- See *everything*—no matter how we are feeling about it—as a chance to become wiser.
- Accept that we need *not* do anything *immediately* about what we understand so we can avoid fear of actions as a resistance to looking further into our lives.
- Always start our reflection with a recall of our own talents and gifts—both the major ones and the ones that rarely see light. This will help us balance the positive with the challenging and see how our gifts can be mobilized to help us with our own shortcomings—especially during difficult times.

In essence, if we see that the process of seeking to understand ourselves better is both fun and helpful to undertake, it will turn out to be more honest, offer a better perspective on life, and help turn bits of understanding into ways of flowing with a more compassionate and richer life. It will also become an end in itself rather than simply a vehicle for self-understanding and beneficial change. The journey, not simply the goal, will be the focus. When this happens, less concern about success and failure and more about faithfulness to a life well lived and experienced will be the result—and that is a result we can truly live with!

40

Personality Styles

Gifts and Deficits

> I believe my house is haunted. Every time I look in the mirror a crazy old lady stands in front of me so I can't see my reflection.
>
> —Anonymous

> Be yourself. Everyone else is already taken.
>
> —Oscar Wilde

As I look at my friends, there are many with amazing personality styles who make me want to jump up and down and be grateful for their presence in my life. However, such friends are so gifted because they excel at a particular style. And so, to expect that they will have a gift that others in our circle of friends might have is unrealistic. It is a bit like hot fudge: wonderful on ice cream but not so good on baked beans!

An example of this is the ability some people have to be present in such an undiluted way when they are with us. When we are in their midst, it is an amazing experience. They are just stunning in their ability to make us feel we are the center of their universe . . . and we are *at that moment.*

As in any such fantastic gift, however, there is always a downside. We need to be aware of this so we don't have expectations that are unrealistic for them. For instance, in the case of people who truly are present to us when we are together, we must recognize that when we are not in their orbit, we may be almost totally forgotten. This is not a negative critique. After all, think it through: How is it possible for someone to be completely present if they thought of others when they were with us? The problem becomes evident when you are in the category of "other" because they are in the presence of someone else. It is not that we are less important. We are just not there. Think about it with respect to those who don't have the gift of "presence." They are not as present to us because their mind is wandering, caught in the past or thinking of the future. Quite simply, we can't have it both ways.

And so, the results of knowing this reality are the following:

- We can truly enjoy the heart of the personality style of others and not be upset at their downside when we know and accept it.
- We can also begin to truly appreciate *our own* gifts and understand both their benefit and challenge to others without taking offense if they feel put off by us when they expect what we cannot do for them and don't understand when we don't meet certain needs that they see as natural for us to be able to fill.

One of the roles of seeking greater self-understanding is to fathom the depth of the primary gifts or signature strengths of our personality style. It is also an opportunity to explore lesser talents to see if they are being given the attention they need. Otherwise, they run the risk of going unnoticed, forgotten, or remaining undeveloped. Furthermore, self-mentoring also includes a time to reflect on the gifts of other persons in our circle of friends as well. In this way, we can enjoy them and not be put off because they don't also have additional gifts that we wish they did have.

Sounds simple. But often we don't give enough attention to the reality of only "being human" and, as a result, pay an unnecessary psychological price for it.

41

Becoming an Elder . . . Not Simply Older

> Do not grow old, no matter how long you live. Never cease to stand like curious children before the great mystery into which we were born.
>
> —Albert Einstein

> What an elder saw while sitting, a youth could not see while standing.
>
> —African Proverb

There are persons I grew up with whom I have lost contact for many years. Then, in an unexpected phone call, chance meeting, or email, we are in each other's presence again!

The joy in reconnecting is amazing. (I'm even smiling right now as I write this.) In my own case, when such informal "reunions" occur, memories flood back, soon laughter is often contagious between the two of us, and I think both of us are surprised in the moment at how much we can remember from the distant past—whether it actually happened or not!

With a number of these friends from childhood, before long the exchange starts to falter. In response, we ask perfunctory questions about family activities, work, etc. We then go our separate ways with vague promises to reconnect. Immediately after hanging up, the past returns to its proper place: present in some way but almost forgotten.

Still, with some of these old friends, the relationship is rekindled and not simply returned to the psychological shelf from where it was retrieved after all these years. The reason for the difference? These friends have not become frozen in, and idols of, the distant past. They recall and rejoice in many joint experiences like others from our past but with one significant difference: They are not captured by the past. They didn't stop growing.

I have also seen this in professionals. For instance, after 30 years some psychotherapists don't have 30 years of experience to share . . . they mainly have 30 years of *practicing* what they knew when they started clinical work. They haven't constantly sought to unlearn and let go so they could seek to learn anew. They also fail to appreciate the importance of humility, at any age, in any role, even with the honorific title ("Doctor") they may have received upon graduation.

With mentoring ourselves, on the other hand, once again there is an honoring of the spiritual and psychological creed:

> When you take knowledge and add humility you get wisdom.
>
> When you take this very wisdom and add it to compassion for others and yourself, you get Love.

It is this sense of love that is at the heart of life. It is also the very reason some of us will become an elder who can share true wisdom with others, whereas others will simply become older and frozen at some past stage. When we choose to have the courage and commitment to both the Spirit and process of self-mentoring, it is the wisdom of the elder and embrace of true love that we should seek.

For this to occur, we must

- take out some quiet time for mindfulness in the moment;
- surface the objective occurrences—*what* happened during the day;
- tend to the subjective—*how* we felt about what happened;
- uncover the underlying thoughts, perceptions, and understandings that led to the feelings we have and the possible subsequent actions and reactions we feel we should take;
- correct misconceptions and dysfunctional thinking; and
- reframe our interpretations so they are more accurate and helpful rather than discouraging and distracting from living a peaceful, meaningful life going forward.

It is important to honor the *spirit* of self-mentoring by seeking to embrace the values of humility, honesty, clarity, kindness, character, and compassion (including *self*-compassion). When we do this, we become the elder we are called to be for others rather than practicing past approaches while simply growing older. Our choices and effort regarding this can have a potentially major impact both on our lives and on those who come into our world. And so, understanding the process of reflection, debriefing ourselves, and self-understanding, as outlined briefly here, is not simply an intellectual exercise . . . it is a potentially life-changing understanding of ourselves and our perception of the people in our lives and world in which we live.

42

"Look Who's Talking!"

Whenever I tease one of my friends about his behavior, he often responds by saying, "Look who's talking!" as a way of somewhat deflecting the veiled criticism. At some level, it is also a reminder to me that I need to more closely and accurately look at my own behavior as well. However, when there is no one around and I criticize myself without thinking whether it is accurate or not, there is no one to say to me, "Look who's talking!"

An accurate understanding of the source and accuracy of our own self-talk can have a quite dramatic positive impact on increasing our understanding of how we view ourselves and the world. Moreover, when we question ourselves further with greater care, we are less apt to fall prey to distortions in our thinking, understanding, and perception of ourselves and life. We can also discover how some of our unexamined beliefs and thoughts have driven us in the wrong direction and resulted in negative feelings that weren't deserved. Our whole life can become richer when we don't waste psychic energy on worry, self-blame, and defensiveness because we can see through the distorted, negative thinking "simply" because we took the time and energy to look further when we felt uneasy or upset.

Psychotherapists, coaches, and guides do this type of questioning as a matter of course for those who come to them. In self-mentoring, we can also follow suit and bring home the power to change life by asking ourselves questions such as the following:

- When angry: Why am I making myself so upset in this situation?
- When worried: What is it that I fear losing?
- When feeling deprived: What is it that I am demanding of others and the world as a price for my happiness?
- When feeling intensely concerned about an outcome: What is the worst thing that could happen if this occurs?
- When wasting a great deal of energy on trying to control life: How can I discern what I can and can't control so I can both conserve and employ my limited energy wisely?
- When I feel lonely: How can I separate being alone and feeling lonely through understanding what is changing solitude into feelings of abandonment?
- When I get very upset over something small: How and why am I taking an annoying event and changing it into something worse?

Such questions are among the type that helps us become freer and more powerful. They break the mental habit of having unrealistic or distorted thoughts, expectations, fears, angers, anxieties, and stress. They also encourage a spirit of intrigue as we ask questions that can produce wonderful information on how we are living. In addition, they can unmask information on how we may be falling into patterns of pleasing, grasping, and seeking to control the uncontrollable.

So, why don't we all do this and live more richly with greater compassion, inner peace, and joy? Why don't we challenge ourselves by saying, "Look who's talking!" when we are thinking in a particular way so we can see life and ourselves more clearly?

Well, as in seeing anything true, there is a price: humility and honesty. We must face our gifts and our growing edges with a sense of *equanimity* to learn what is holding us back. This may not be easy, but it is quite simple and rewarding once we seriously undertake it with an attitude of gentle acceptance—especially during difficult times.

43

What You Already Know . . . Is the Problem

Most people are concerned about their *lack* of knowledge. They worry about what they need to know that will help them respond to situations. Although, at some level, this makes sense, what is not recognized is that new mental space is needed for such learning to take place. And so, an even more insidious danger to obtaining wisdom is a lack of enough humility to recognize that more dangerous than the ignorance we are aware of is what we *think* we already know but actually don't.

Seeing that we are wrong is very difficult for some people and a task for the rest of us. Indian psychologist and spiritual writer, Anthony DeMello, knew this. He teased people about how "hard hearted" some of us could be and that all of us were with certain issues and people. To illustrate this, in a presentation, he shared the following story, which begins when a woman suddenly crosses the street to stop a man she saw and says,

> "Henry, I am so happy to see you after all these years! My, how you have changed."
>
> "I remember you as being tall and you seem so much shorter now."
>
> "You used to have a pale complexion and it is really so ruddy now."
>
> "Good grief how you have changed in five years!"

> Finally, the man got a chance to interject, "But my name is not Henry!"
>
> To which the persistent woman calmly responded, "Oh, so you have changed your name too!"

We have absorbed a great deal of information throughout the years. When we sit with a mentor, we are questioned upon what we are basing certain beliefs and cognitions. The goal is to uncover information that is false, exaggerated, prejudiced, or no longer accurate now. The aim is to allow us to become more open to new realities and possibilities about ourselves as well as the way we view others and the world.

There is so much blocking us from seeing clearly because of traditions in our family, personal habits, and societal norms that may not be life-giving. Also, much of the information we hold onto is quite vague. It subtly impacts how we think and behave, so it is difficult to catch ourselves in the act of misrepresenting reality.

Two key elements can help in this regard. One is to be as *detailed* as possible as to why we believe, think, or react the way we do. To do this, we must question ourselves further rather than accepting what initially makes sense to us. To a psychotherapy patient I was treating, I asked, "What do you think made you so angry at this person?" She responded quite vehemently, "Well, wouldn't *you* become angry at him?" She was obviously now angry at me.

Rather than responding in kind, I simply said,

> Well, if you and I left the building together and something happened across the street that I interpreted in such a way that I really become furious, it is totally conceivable that you wouldn't view it the same way. It would then be natural for you to ask me, "What's going on? Why are you so angry?" This would force me to take a look at what it was touching within me that was causing a response different than yours.

To be able to recognize the need to question ourselves in this way, however, we must be willing to embrace a virtue or signature strength that is not very popular today: *humility*. Yet, it might help if we realized that it is important to recognize that seeing things clearly through the lens of honesty deepens us as persons and also can give space to others and enliven relationships.

44

Friendship's True Gift

> Loneliness does not come from having no people around you, but from being unable to communicate the things that seem important to you.
>
> —Carl Jung

A number of years ago, I treated a very bright person who I felt also brought out the best in me. And so, I felt challenged when he called and asked for a last-minute appointment because all I had to offer was a spot at the end of the day. I am not a "night person," so I knew I would not be at the top of my game.

When he did arrive, I was truly not my best. I knew that I would not be able to provide the "sterling feedback" and interpretations I felt I had succeeded in making in past therapy sessions. My pride was on the line—and for someone with a large ego like myself, this was a bit challenging.

As the session went on, I realized I was even worse than I thought. I could "only" listen. Given my lack of energy, I had enough of a job simply staying in tune with the story he was sharing. And so, my reformulated goal in this session, unlike the others, was to listen carefully so as to store up information for the following session when I thought I would be more alert and articulate.

And so, we spent almost the entire session with him sharing a poignant story about a morning encounter that he had which didn't go well for him. I said very little as he energetically told what had happened as well as how he perceived it, the feelings it brought to the fore, and how it triggered shame in him. (With energy like he had, he was obviously a "night person.")

Finally, I noticed that our time was about up and mentioned this as a way of preparing him to wrap up the story he was telling at that point. In response, he said, "May I just finish this part of it?" I nodded affirmatively and said, "Of course."

When he did finish, he stood up, smiled, and thanked me for squeezing him in at the end of the day. "Glad to be able to do it, Jack," I replied.

He then went over to the door to leave—and I'll never forget this—turned around at the last moment and said to me, "You know what, doc? I think this is the *best* session we've ever had!"

What we often don't realize as persons in the helping profession or friends to those who turn to us for support is that the true gift of a relationship is the ability to "just" *listen*—as opposed to remaining quiet while waiting for our opportunity to speak.

Listening, at its core, gives space to persons so they can "air" what they are feeling so strongly about. More than feedback, empathy, or sympathy—which all have important roles to be sure—people need a chance to tell their story. It is in the sharing of their dreams, fears, angers, worries, joys, and visions that a good relationship is formed. But who gets to do that today?

I shared with a senior colleague that one of my patients was having difficulty in terminating therapy. I told him that we had reformulated our goals several times and in each case met them, but she still wanted to come in.

In response, he smiled and said,

> Why the surprise on your part? Where can many of us go where the person *actually* listens to us? Moreover, when people leave the therapy session, they often experience a psychological and spiritual relapse because many in their world cannot get out of themselves enough to listen.

These events were to come back to me when I, myself, went into mentoring and the person I was seeing asked if there was a specific reason or problem for my visit. I remember replying, "No. Nothing dramatic is going on." I was coming to see him so I could simply share my story, be listened to nonjudgmentally, and occasionally be given feedback on what I had shared—which is no easy thing in today's world.

I saw this more and more as my meetings continued. I realized that in addition to the listening he had done and the balanced clear, kind feedback he occasionally offered, there was another essential step he was modeling for me to take. The true gift of his listening to me was also an encouragement for modeling how I must then *listen to myself.*

I realized that in mentoring myself, I needed to more carefully listen to my own feelings, thoughts, perceptions, and ways of understanding in the same way my mentor and other good friends do for me. However, to accomplish this, I needed to value "alone time" where I could have the space both to see the objective—*what* happened—and to fathom the subjective—*how* I reacted to these events so I could better appreciate my inner reactions and subsequent actions.

That is why when I hear someone say, "Oh, I only 'just listened,'" I stop them and ask, "When is the last time someone truly listened to you like you listened to others?"

When someone truly listens, it is a gift that provides an opportunity to discover anew a sense of perspective, new vision, hope, a sense of belonging, and, maybe, for the first time in a long while, a smile on your face. Friends who listen can help do that . . . so can it happen when we are enough of a friend to ourselves to listen to what is going on within *ourselves* as well.

45

Isn't It Nice to Understand?

> Thinking is difficult, that's why most people judge.
>
> —Carl Jung

> Do not judge by appearances; a rich heart may be under a poor coat.
>
> —Scottish proverb

One of the most powerful potential teachings of a crisis, trauma, loss, or unusual event such as a pandemic is that we can no longer live by the same rhythm as we have in the past. Living as we may have habitually done in the past may actually be a detriment. If we don't learn this lesson, and it is possible to resist accepting this teaching, we are simply turning down the gifts being offered at each subsequent juncture in life—including the period during a crisis.

In a crisis, the primary call is to wake up to living life differently than we have in the past. Even if the past and our style of living then were wonderful, the psychological and spiritual scenery is changed . . . so *we* must change. I remember lecturing in Thailand and watching new arrivals from the West running around as if they were in northern Montana taking no note of the heat and humidity of Bangkok. The result? They became overheated and dehydrated as well as totally exhausted by noon. They were no longer in Montana but refused to accept this fact. Is Montana lovely? *Absolutely!* But they were now in Thailand. The same needs to be recognized by us when our psychological terrain changes after a loss or amidst serious stress. In addition, as in the case of the person arriving in Thailand, if he slowed down a bit, he might enjoy his surroundings a bit more. Bangkok is truly an amazing place to slowly savor.

Dramatic changes may bring us to therapy, psychological coaching, or spiritual guidance. It is good to treat yourself to such support when in the midst of significant transitions. But, whether this step is taken or not, it certainly must bring us to self-mentor ourselves more clearly and less emotionally at such times. For instance, after making a small or large mistake in our lives, guilt doesn't help because it doesn't call us to change but instead freezes us in the past. Likewise, anxiety doesn't prepare us for the future—it merely fills the present so we are not open to be truly alert so we cannot enjoy and learn from what is happening before us "in the now."

But, true understanding—ah, that is something entirely different. It doesn't look at the past in a way that is harmful or as a way to make believe it didn't happen. No. Instead, it tries to see its impact so it can no longer dominate us now or stain the future so much that it can't be lived in a better spirit, with a stronger ethic, and with greater peace and joy.

Understanding also is a model of cognitive balance—we think more clearly about ourselves and life because we are not only seeking clarity about our weaknesses, flaws, and failures but also seeking to uncover our strengths. More and more we know who we are as persons when we can combine true excitement over our talents and gifts with an honest sense of our shortcomings. It is the humility that arises out of playing to our strengths while acknowledging our weaknesses or defenses.

Mentoring yourself is a bit like mining. The way we do it is by shining a psychological beacon on the hidden inner "ore" in ourselves that may have remained concealed until now. The psychological and spiritual helmet light that shines the way for us to achieve this in "cognitive and emotional caves of darkness" includes

- helpful feedback from others ... plus our willingness to entertain it;
- the words of sages from books we have read;
- a willingness to reframe darkness so we can see what it might offer us that success and other so-called "positive" experiences can't; and

- an openness to look further and not stop searching for more elements of the truth about ourselves and life—even ones that we may not like, such as someday we will die.

One of the other such self-mentoring mining approaches is to be open to ask honest, sometimes different or painful questions of ourselves, such as the following:

- What is my basic style of dealing with the world?
- What are the gifts that most people recognize in me?
- What are some of the lesser gifts that I need to give more attention to developing and sharing?
- When do I "trip over" my gifts because of a sense of insecurity, defensiveness, or anxiety?
- What are some comments I hate to hear about myself?
- What makes me most happy? Anxious? Peaceful? Stressed? Angry?
- What are the types of persons I most dislike?
- What are some of the ways I refuse the love that is already around me?
- How do I follow up on good ideas?
- What are some ways that I can open up more opportunities for what I like and how can I be more qualitatively compassionate toward others?
- In what ways do I welcome new possibilities, provide time for ideas and visions to develop, and value creativity and spontaneity?

Such questions, and the general "psychological and spiritual mining" we do, are helped immeasurably by taking a few moments at the end of the day to write them down in a journal. Also, essential to a good self-mentoring process and relationship is taking out time in silence and solitude on a regular basis each day. Having a refreshing space to relax, renew, be present, mindful, and possibly meditate is the key to appreciating the defining days during difficult times. In this way, they don't simply interrupt our lives but instead provide the opportunity for new growth, peace, and joy that weren't possible before.

46

The Holocaust and the Joy of a Healthy Perspective

When I think of maintaining a healthy perspective during these days of lockdown, angry posts, and divisive politics, my memory is drawn back to two events from the Holocaust that I have read about. They made me stop, fill up, be grateful for all that I have, and marvel at the resilience of good people.

The first story is from *All But My Life: A Memoir* by Gerda Weissman Klein, a holocaust survivor of the Sobibor extermination camp:

> Ilse, a childhood friend of mine, once found a raspberry in the concentration camp and carried it in her pocket all day to present to me that night on a leaf. Imagine a world in which your entire possession is one raspberry and you give it to your friend?

This story reminded me of a different story of how horribly the inmates at another concentration camp were treated. However, when they returned after a day of dehumanization and impossible work, a stray dog that had gotten into the camp became so excited to see them, and wagged his tail vigorously, that he, rather than the "human beings" running the camp, reflected for the prisoners that they were worth a great deal as persons.

I share these two stories not as "downers" since most people are going through a great deal today. However, I believe they can help me and you realize more keenly how precious life is, how much we have to enjoy, and call us to try to be gentle and not react negatively to those who would share or post angry or sarcastic words. This doesn't mean that we shouldn't reply and stand up for what we believe is right. Being neutral as Elie Wiesel would remind us is tantamount to siding with what is evil or wrong. Still, how we respond is important, so we don't add psychological gasoline to the fires of others' anger that is merely covering their fears and hurts.

The choice to have a healthy perspective and do what we can to bring people together is up to us. When it is done in the right way, as some have learned who experienced posttraumatic growth, our efforts aren't as depleting and may, in a strange way, actually strengthen us as well in the process.

47

Standing in the Darkness

> You don't have to sit outside in the dark. If, however, you wish to look at the stars, you will find the darkness is necessary.
>
> —Annie Dillard
> *Teaching a Stone to Talk*

During a presentation to ministers, a lecturer asked an intended rhetorical question: "What do you think is the core of your work?" But before he could proceed, surprisingly one of the clerics in the audience yelled out, "Helping people through the night." The same can also be said of physicians, nurses, psychologists, social workers, counselors, relief workers/nongovernmental workers, educators, others in the helping and healing professions, and really anyone of us who take on a caring role.

For more than 30 years, the primary focus of my work has been to supervise, mentor, teach, and treat persons in these professional roles. As they walked with others in the darkness, I journeyed with them—especially when as professionals they became lost, discouraged, disillusioned, or traumatized due to the work in which they were involved (what we now call "secondary stress").

As well as individual work with these helpers, much of my efforts also involved delivering presentations to varied groups of caregivers on resilience, self-care, and how to maintain a healthy perspective. I also often addressed the general public because all of us are required to be caregivers of some type at different times in our lives.

In the United States, I was privileged to speak at such venues as Walter Reed Army Hospital and at a commemoration of the 2013 Boston Marathon bombing, as well as in such areas abroad as Beirut, Phnom Penh, Belfast, Guatemala City, Haiti, Cape Town, Budapest, Hanoi, and other places where caregivers were experiencing great professional stress and personal anxiety. In these settings, I was impressed not only by the challenges these helpers and healers were facing but also even more so by their openness, humility, and willingness to let go when the percept they were holding onto, which was causing them so much pain, was challenged.

For instance, after a presentation in South Africa to those involved in caring for the poor, a social worker raised her hand to get my attention. When I asked her if she had a question, she exclaimed, "I can't do it anymore. I need to leave the profession . . . now!"

"What exactly is the nature of your work?" I asked.

She responded,

> I help women who have been raped or abused. They are poor and usually single parents. When I go with them to court, they must take a day off from work, which they can ill afford. Then when we get there the judge—who is usually male—often looks at the papers we hand him, shrugs, makes a face, and says, "I haven't had time to look over the case yet. Make another appointment." It is just so discouraging. What I do is useless. I am useless.

I let the emotion in the moment settle for a time. Then, after a period of quiet, I said to her, "Given what you have told me, I have a few questions for you. First, who else was with this woman during her time of desolation?"

"Only me."

"Would it be an overstatement to say at that moment you were emotionally closer to her than anyone else in the world?"

She paused for a moment and answered in a hoarse voice, "No it wouldn't be. She had only me. There was no one else."

In response, I looked at her, and in as gentle a voice as I could muster, asked, "And, you want to leave that?" Then, after another period of quiet tearfulness on her part, I added,

> We all make the mistake of focusing solely on apparent success. But, it is not success that matters. It is personal and professional faithfulness. We should never underestimate the power of faithfulness even though the world might tell us it is only immediate desired results that matter.

Not just helpers need to hear this—everyone does. Parents often feel lost when their children go astray even though they have done their best to help their children traverse the psychological deserts of life that young people must face and cross as part of growing up. In marriages, spouses often lose their way when marital problems arise and seem to overwhelm them. When the workplace turns toxic for any of us, the lessons that all caregivers must learn if they are to remain vital are also relevant to all of our situations.

What professional helpers and healers learn at some point if they want to continue to remain as faithful guides is that how they view their care for others, especially when it is most challenging, is a crucial factor. As I have mentioned in four previous books (*Night Call: Embracing Compassion and Hope in a Troubled World*; *Bounce: Living the Resilient Life*; *Perspective: The Calm Within the Storm*; and *Riding the Dragon: 10 Lessons for Inner Strength in Challenging Times*), self-care, maintaining a healthy perspective, learning approaches to expanding one's resiliency range, and understanding the importance of self-renewal all help in this regard. However, beyond this, there are wonderful simple, powerful lessons worth being appreciated anew by all of us on how to enjoy a more rewarding life. In this regard, I have found that even in some of the passing encounters experienced in the work I do, there have been "whispers" of a meaningful way to approach our brief time on this earth. I believe they are worth knowing so all of us—no matter what our role in life is—can appreciate them anew.

Putting them into practice will take both reflection and practice. Yet, as Annie Dillard aptly remarks in her book, *The Writing Life*, "There is no shortage of good days. It is good lives that are hard to come by." Yes, she's right . . . but it is all worth the right type of efforts to make it so.

48

Simple Graciousness

> They may forget what you said but they will never forget how you made them feel.
>
> —Carl W. Beuhner

In a workshop I gave a number of years ago to helpers in Cambodia, I had a chance to take a break in Phnom Penh. From what I could sense, the workshop was going fairly well thus far. However, after the first day, I was still feeling the stress of performance anxiety. And so, as I suggest to others experiencing stress, I decided to take a walk, in this case, along the Mekong River. I also toured the main Buddhist temple, whose walls were still pockmarked with bullet holes. As I was doing this, I heard a noise and looked up only to see that the skies had suddenly darkened in preparation for the brief but drenching storms that would move through the area at this time of year.

As I was thinking about where to seek shelter, it began to rain, lightly at first but then quite heavily. I was caught out in the open and thought, "Ah, well" when I saw in the distance a Khmer shopkeeper waving me over to take shelter with him. In response, I ran over to his "establishment," which really was a stall consisting of just a couple of tables of goods with an overhang that shielded shoppers from the bright sun or, in this case, the heavy rain.

By the time I got to him, even though it was a brief sprint, the rains were really coming down. As I approached, I saw him pat a section of the table with his left hand and smile at me broadly as if to nonverbally say, "Come sit by me." In return, I nodded my head because I knew only a few words of Khmer and he, as I would discover, knew some French but no English. We sat together quietly. He didn't seem concerned about his loss of business because of the weather, and I was in no hurry to go anywhere else. During the remainder of the few hours' break I had left, I had only a planned visit to a small museum on my list.

The rain was gone in about 20 minutes, but the positive results for me felt surprisingly amazing. Thinking about the man's spontaneous compassion, his ease at taking an unexpected break in his work, and his appreciation of my smile and expression of gratitude as I joined together the tips of my hands and gestured toward him as I got up to leave made me appreciate a positive undercurrent of simplicity in his life and our interaction.

In walking away, I thought to myself, I want to possess more deeply that type of simple graciousness the shopkeeper gave to someone he did not know and who could not do anything for him. I wanted this attitude even though I knew that it was so often scorned by a society that keeps score on what is given out in order to ensure it is returned in measure or with interest. While many multimillionaires would respond with scorn at the idea that their social security payments be lessened so the poor could have more, this man with so little shared what he had with me. Moreover, he didn't do it out of guilt or duty but, rather, because it was the natural thing for him to do at that time.

Giving and expecting nothing in return are true graciousness, and it seemed to make him happy too! I wanted that attitude, so I kept the experience midbrain in the hope that I could understand it more fully. But, as I was to find out, giving of yourself takes opening yourself up and recognizing when egoism plays interference with receiving and accepting life as it is.

49

Leaning Back to Find Openness, Possibility . . . and a Healthy Perspective

During the height of the sexual abuse crisis, I was asked by the Roman Catholic Archdiocese of Boston to speak to the priests about navigating psychological and spiritual darkness. The final group I was asked to address was a group of retired clergy. They were in an especially tough spot because just prior to my arrival, someone whom they respected and trusted was also accused of being an abuser. Knowing this, I tried to be both informative and gentle. As with all the persons I treat or mentor, I wanted to balance kindness with clarity.

Just as I was completing the question and answer period and was getting ready to leave the stage, a kindly elderly priest whom I had a chance to chat with during one of the breaks raised his hand. Seeing it, I recognized him and asked, "Father, did you have a question or comment you wished to make?"

In response, he said, "I would like to divinize you for the moment." I replied, "That sounds dangerous!" and there was a ripple of laughter in the room. However, he went on in a very serious vein. "Given all we have been through these past few years, can you predict when this will all end?"

The room was suddenly very silent and I, myself, paused at the poignancy and import of this question. Finally, after some time, I replied, "Father, even if I knew the answer to that question, I wouldn't answer it." "Why?" he asked in a puzzled voice.

"Because it is the wrong question."Then, after waiting a few heartbeats, I added, "The question is not, 'When will it all end?'The question is, 'What can I learn from all of this?'"

With the proper awareness, experiences of failure, distress, loss, and trauma can lead us to generative actions for others rather than being more involved only in ourselves to the point where we lose a healthy perspective. Examples are present in everyday people who are not psychotherapists or clinicians of some type.

In Ishinomaki, Japan, after the tsunami, a person who was relocated into a shelter soon after his own house became uninhabitable, almost immediately started sweeping out the shelter where he was crammed in with others. When asked why he did this, he replied, "No one should live like this. I just do better when I am helping other people." The point? Compassion has a place in being resilient—not simply after the fact but during it.

In the Waldo Canyon disaster in Colorado, a resident first exclaimed upon looking at the rubble that stood in place of his house, "I have lost everything!" And then, after some time, he added, "No, I have lost my home of 30 years and all my physical possessions and this makes me sad, but I have not lost my life."The point? Developing a healthy perspective is part of resilience.

In another case, a priest who was called to a hospital to meet with parents of twins, one who was born dead, said,

> When we first went to the morgue to pray over the shrouded child who had died, we cried and prayed. Then we went up to the neonatal intensive care unit and prayed beside the twin that had survived. We cried and prayed again but this time they were prayers of joy which I don't think I could have done had I not first cried those tears of sadness.

The point? We don't gain a new perspective or deeper sense of gratitude for what is truly important in life by avoiding the sadness, trauma, or loss but by facing it directly with a sense of openness and possibility.

Examples such as these, then, require that we simultaneously appreciate the dangers of involvement with others while appreciating the meaning and personal return of doing it. A key problem is that because we are drawn to care for others in a professional or personal way, we set ourselves up. The seeds of personal burnout and the seeds of compassion are, in reality, the same seeds. Although we don't wish to be callous and I am not recommending that (we have enough callous people in the world already!), over-involvement with the emotions or expectations of others can prevent us from doing the very tasks we want to do for friends, family, or, in the case of professionals, clients or patients. The opposite of having some emotional distance from others is not compassion but seduction. We are pulled in by the tension or upset of the moment and then are of limited use to the person we are trying to help.

There is a Russian proverb that captures the situation being described here: "When you sleep next to the cemetery, you can't cry for everyone who dies." Leaning back from the emotions experienced by others under stress, after loss, or following trauma is part of a triad: We lean back, reappraise, and then renew so we can re-enter the fray with new energy and understanding.

50

A Refreshing Place of My Own

> [A person] cannot long survive without air, water, and sleep. Next in importance comes food. And close on its heels, solitude.
>
> —Thomas Szasz
> *The Second Sin*

> I was lonely because I had no experience with solitude. I never realized I had been given a gift; I didn't know how to use the great present of time alone.
>
> —Doris Grumbach
> *Fifty Days of Solitude*

Many people envision "right" vacation spots for inner renewal. Maybe it is a place on the ocean, a lake, in the mountains, or even a bustling city because, as some will quip, "I stay away from being out in the country because I am afraid of grass and trees."

Yet, the true, constant refreshing place that all of us have in common and share access to is quiet, possibly alone time, within ourselves. Although, for a number of reasons, we rarely go there even though it can provide a refreshing space like no other.

To avoid this spacious area of freedom, living in the moment, gentle breathing, and relaxing with one's eyes closed or lightly setting them on something before you, is unfortunately quite common today. Even when some do avail themselves of it, they manage to spoil the potential tenor of the milieu by making the whole thing into a project rather than an experience greeted with no expectations, just loving attention and a generosity of spirit.

If there should be a goal at all, it is coming home to yourself. This animates self-mentoring so it can be transformed from self-improvement to a true sense of self love that stands apart from narcissism, on the one hand, and inordinate self-criticism, on the other hand.

Taking time in silence and solitude is not a luxury. It is a central part of being human. Even distractions can be instructive if you let the alone time rest lightly. This is done by avoiding entertaining what comes up or, on the other hand, trying to suppress anything. Instead, see what arises as if you are riding on a train and viewing the passing terrain.

Fear that we will learn unpleasant realities about ourselves, which are easier to ignore during activity or interaction with others, prevents people from sitting long enough. If that isn't enough of a resistance to giving oneself some space, then boredom is a convincer that it is all useless and that we can spend the time better by *doing* something.

But alone time is neither a period for us to beat ourselves up and condemn others nor an evasion of life. How could it be if some time in quiet apart does the following?

- Allows all the defensive facades to crumble so we can see inside our life *as it is* in order to appreciate what is authentic and what is lived out because others mirror rules for us to follow or offer us bribes to live that way
- Provides useful information about our ordinary selves that allows us to see how society or family has convinced us to contradict our true selves—often said to be in our best interest
- Helps us find truths that can buoy and teach us when we need it most
- Uncovers old, hidden stories that are quietly chaining us to the past so we can't claim the copyright to who we believe we are, and can be, with a bit more information and freedom to relax with and think for ourselves
- Reveals limits others have placed at our mental doorstep that we absorbed long ago under the rubric of respect
- Offers us a chance to lose the psychological and spiritual weight of unnecessary worry, anger, resentment, anxiety, stress, guilt, and blame so we can find what is good in life

Silence and solitude can make our days feel longer and more meaningful. They stop us from running to our grave believing that mindlessly taking care of numerous tasks equals a "full" life. Instead, alone time can help us "graduate" into living reflectively and feeling more centered so we can flow rather than drift through our day.

Mentoring ourselves requires that we take our day gently and attentively so we can be present to life while it is still flowing through our veins. The narrative of our life is forfeited if we avoid truly being with ourselves. The chance to encounter the peace and joy and gifted identity may be buried under all the psychological and spiritual noise around and within us.

Quiet time is certainly worth taking the trip behind all the screens blocking close contact with life. As a matter of fact, silence and solitude may help in the actual enjoyment of being with others and listening to music or checking the messages received on our computers because we will be freer, more attentive, and integrated persons when we do make contact. Now, that's *living*!

Epilogue

> Don't play the notes, play the *meaning* of the notes.
>
> —Pablo Casals

> Sometimes the easiest way to solve a problem is to stop participating in the problem.
>
> —Albert Einstein

> Don't wish me happiness. I don't expect to be happy all the time . . . Wish me courage and strength and a sense of humor. I will need them all.
>
> —Anne Morrow Lindberg

The activity of mentoring ourselves is designed to help us appreciate who we are in less general, superficial terms. When most people see us, it is more or less a one-dimensional view. They find a dominant trait and, if we are lucky, they decorate it a bit with a few more of our gifts and psychological blemishes to make us more interesting. If we are not careful, after a while we also may begin to view ourselves in similar ways.

Sometimes, it takes a helpful stranger—therapist, spiritual guide, or coach—to lead us deeper. It may be to encourage us not to be afraid to take another, more careful look and to move away from the place our family, friends, and society may want us to remain. This type of guide enables us to gently ask ourselves to be a bit more open to new possibilities, stop catastrophizing if we are not in the place others would have us be, and move ahead from the past as well as to stop merely fantasizing about the magic that might happen in the future that will save us.

Such helpful persons enable us to be practical but also see beyond only the "lyrics" (tasks) of daily life and its constant demands. They move us to honor the "music" of life: beauty, friendship, kindness, love, meaning, gratitude, and humor. This is done through mindful attention, a non-morbid appreciation of our vulnerability and eventual death, and a sense that everything can teach and call us deeper—even, *especially*, during difficult times.

In mentoring ourselves, we seek to build on the ways that other wisdom figures have treated us. This isn't an improved version of who we believe we are now or even an "advanced copy" of how we are reflected in an interpersonal mirror. It is truly a willingness to fathom broader aspects of ourselves so we cease to be unidimensional. And to accomplish this, we begin to grasp that the process of mentoring ourselves is a journey in which questions keep changing and life ceases to be a fixed fact. It is a psychological trip upstream against the common current of habit and societal values that may not be ours.

We begin to recognize the dangers of being in an interpersonal boat in which many of those around us may be satisfied with existing as they are or are constantly complaining but feel they have no choice as victims of life's turns. We also appreciate the fact that even when everyone in the boat may be pleased with the view of the psychological and spiritual landscape . . . from our vantage point, it can be going in the *wrong* direction!

And so, while a crisis, trauma, or pandemic in such interpersonal settings may be seen as solely a setback or period of waiting for "normal" to return, when we seek to mentor ourselves, the goal is a further awakening that might not have been possible if life as usual was not abruptly and possibly horribly interrupted.

Given this, regular periods of silence and solitude were encouraged in this book as a necessary, quiet path to a surprising, more aware encounter with life by providing space to draw experiences out of life based on a new way of looking at it. Yet, mentoring ourselves isn't simply a way of finding new ideas, although they will arise during alone time. It is nothing less than moving out of our cognitive envelope in which we are thinking even as we walk along the beach or through a park surrounded by welcoming beauty, so making all things new becomes more possible.

When this occurs, we are opening the door wider to awe, being unpretentious, experiencing a new calm as we move away from the mirror of others' opinions of us, and freeing ourselves from freezing the frames in life. The result is a new rhythm in life less marked by habit and more in keeping with the need to flow with who and what is in front of us now. It is also actually animated by the many detours from society's false preoccupation with security, comfort, and pleasure that too many claim are the stated requirements for happiness.

When this happens, questions start to pop up—no longer in the form of personal recrimination for our failures or anger from others for not meeting their needs the way they want them met, but as simple oases from going along with the rules for happiness that are not applicable to living with meaning anymore. They are questions that we nonjudgmentally ask of ourselves, as we would directions from someone along the roadside when we are lost.

In doing this, mentoring ourselves allows us to explore the past, fully relish the present, and see a path forward to the future—*our* future. Moreover, in the process, we raise the possibility of enhancing life—not simply for us but also for the world we touch. This not only refers to our close circle of friends or family. It also may be contained in a comment made to a person sitting next to us on a plane or train, a line written in a thank-you note to a distant relative, or in the attitude we carry with us into a local store or restaurant.

When we seek to mentor ourselves, the goal is simple. We seek to find and embrace the truth in a way that we and others blossom; become more resilient; use the same compassion toward ourselves that we extend toward others; and value gaining, regaining, and maintaining a healthy perspective toward life. I think having such an attitude led American Polish classical pianist, Arthur Rubenstein, to say, "Even when I'm sick and depressed, I love life." Such an amazing, positive attitude was not present because he didn't have troubles in life. Instead, it grew out of a gratitude for, and attention to, *all* of life. We can see this in another comment made by Rubenstein when he stated, "To be alive, to be able to see, to walk, to have houses, music, paintings—it's all a miracle. I have adopted the technique of living life miracle to miracle."

However, as was indicated in the 50 themes in this book, to reach such self-understanding takes time, patience, and attention. Many are not familiar with this approach in today's fast-paced world. As we have seen in the previous lessons, this can be frustrating. Still, if we appreciate this, we won't turn our back so quickly on the natural blocks to seeing things as they are—not as we wish they were—nor to fabricate them so they fit neatly into a preset belief system.

It is only when we are truly prepared to leap into a fresh view of our own unexamined beliefs that we will find what is blocking understanding life *as it is*. *Our* life. As Peter France, former BBC presenter, points out, "We all hear important truths many times in our lives, but it is only when we are ready for them that they penetrate." Sculptor August Rodin puts it more bluntly in saying, "You know nothing when you are young; that takes time and only slowly."

This is not merely an acquisition of new knowledge but also a letting go of what has been learned in the past that is no longer true or relevant. Spanish essayist Miguel de Unamuno claimed, "Fascism is cured by reading, and racism is cured by traveling." If this is so, I think limited self-understanding is cured by *un*-learning. Everything we do echoes in some way how we are open to, and can meet, new information, people, and events. Yet, the mini-traumas of life often hold us back and freeze us at a time when they happened with people who may not be living in front of us but remain in our minds.

A crisis or difficult or uncertain time can stop us in our tracks. Force us to disrupt habits. Take a breath. Give us the chance to ask anew: Is this how I want to live? Is this who I really am? Is this how I wish to treat others and be treated myself?

COVID-19 and other crises or traumas are obviously not what we should welcome . . . *ever.* However, when they occur and break up the psychological and spiritual ground beneath our feet, we are given a rare chance to look anew at ourselves and life differently, possibly more deeply. And, mentoring ourselves on a daily basis helps us be in a position to welcome wisdom instead of only feeling pulled down by life's demands.

Mentoring ourselves also helps us move through the daily and trauma-driven windows to seeing life through new psychological prisms of love so we are kinder rather than call people names, are more interested in bringing people together rather than dividing them for our benefit, and become more grateful rather than grasping. It is also designed to explore further when we do feel emotional so we can begin looking at how we are thinking, understanding, and perceiving life so we can learn how to replace impressions and prejudice with clear thinking and appreciation of the *entire* situation rather than seeking to take the easy way out.

It also encourages us to have the same empathy toward ourselves. That is what in broad terms mentoring ourselves is all about. The goal is to search for accuracy and to move away from self-attacks and projections of blame that come from defensiveness to a nonjudgmental understanding of ourselves and the world in which we live. Although not easy, the results can powerfully clear the way for the truth . . . and, yes, although it sounds like merely a throw-a-way line today, it is correct and just as powerful as it has ever been . . . *And, the truth shall set you free.*

Finally, one of the major fruits of mentoring ourselves is how we can be present to others in a way that may even be surprising to those close to us who feel they know us best. The most personal and honest way I can illustrate this is in sharing the following letter I wrote to my two granddaughters—one who was entering sophomore year in university and the other entering senior year in high school. I think it is the most apt way I can close a book on mentoring ourselves that is designed to encourage all of us to view our gifts and growing edges clearly and kindly so we are in a position to be generative to others.

LETTER TO MY GRANDDAUGHTERS

I have been very, very fortunate because my life's work has been what I love. For most of my 40 professional years, after graduating from Hahnemann Medical College with my doctorate in Psych, I have supported helpers and healers so they don't burn out. In part of this "mission," I have gotten the chance to speak as well as write on: self-care, avoiding toxic compassion, maintaining a healthy perspective, and learning creative ways to become more and more resilient.

This has brought me to such cities abroad as Hanoi, Budapest, Guatemala City, Edinburgh, Belfast, Valletta in Malta, Toronto, Rome, Paris, and Tokyo. It has also wound up with me speaking at the U.S. Air Force Academy, Harvard, Yale, Princeton Theological Seminary, the Mayo Clinic, and on Capitol Hill.

My books have in total sold over a hundred thousand copies. To let people know about how they might be of help, I have also appeared on television, spoken on the radio, and been interviewed.

Yet, despite these "successes," what I have not mentioned to your Mom or your Grandmother is that I have always felt like a failure. In a quiet moment, I would sit there and feel that I just missed the mark. Sadness would overtake me. And so, what did I do when I felt like that?

Well, the first thing I did was take some quiet time alone—not to lick my wounds but to be quiet and allow myself to be with the universe in the moment. And then, without denying the depth of these dark feelings, I faced my dysfunctional thinking in two ways.

First, I said, "You are crazy! Look at what you have accomplished." This was done to help me regain perspective and see that something I was taught early in life remained as a false belief within me . . . and would remain with me for the rest of my life. Why? Well, I was taught this preverbally, before I could speak, and nonverbally, often by the very people who said they loved me—and I believe they did—but who had issues of their own.

Second, and of greater import, I reminded myself that "success" was fun . . . but faithfulness both professionally and personally to what is good is much, much more important.

Society may not teach or reinforce this but all sound philosophies and religions do.

And so, I share this with you as you move forward in your life so when you feel like a failure, you will not give up but instead lean back, reflect, re-evaluate, renew, and know that commitment to a life of meaning is what it is all about. It truly is.

Love,
Pop Pop

APPENDIX

"Learning Is the Thing for You"

A Month of Minute Reminders

Sometimes we just need a line or two of something someone said or wrote to inspire and open us to new insights. At other times, we may only have a minute to spare before the curtain to the day's frantic activities opens. With this in mind, the following 30 brief reflections, with space for a brief reflection by you, are offered with the hope they will be considered individually over a period of a month.

Some are quotes from known or obscure sources. Others are simple summaries of the lessons that were shared previously in this book. All are brief enough to be remembered and reflected upon during quiet points in each day. They may seed something for the future or make sense out of something right in front of you. It will be difficult to tell which until you actually become involved in this month of minute reflections.

Sometimes discernment doesn't involve going into a corner to think but, rather, taking action to see where it leads you. I wonder whether and where the following thoughts will actually be followed by action in order to open new portals in meaningful, rewarding, and compassionate living.

One thing I do know, as T. H. White in the following brief passage from *The Once and Future King* notes, "Learning is the thing for you":

> "The best thing for being sad," replied Merlyn . . . "is to learn something. That is the only thing that never fails. You may grow old and trembling in your anatomies, you may lie awake at night listening to the disorder of your veins, you may miss your only love, you may see the world around you devastated by evil lunatics, or know your honor trampled in the sewers of baser minds. There is only one thing for it then—to learn. Learn why the world wags and what wags it. That is

the only thing which the mind can never exhaust, never alienated, never be tortured by, never fear or distrust, and never dream of regretting. Learning is the thing for you.

1. It is not the amount of darkness in the world, your country, workplace, family, or even in yourself that matters . . . it is how you stand in that darkness (perspective) that makes all the difference.
2. "Courage comes and goes . . . hold on for the next supply."—Thomas Merton
3. A sign of psychological and spiritual maturity is the ability to mentally hold life's challenges in one hand and its possibilities in the other so as to be open to where everything—including personal darkness—can take you.
4. "By the time the fool has learned the game, the players have dispersed."—Ashanti proverb
5. When you take knowledge and you add humility, you get wisdom. When you take that very wisdom and add it to compassion, you get love. And, love is at the heart of a rich, resilient life.
6. Turning a corner requires patience and perseverance. Similarly, Anne Wilson Schaff notes, "Recovery is a process, not an event."
7. "The only way out is through."—Helen Keller
8. Staying informed is good; being *overwhelmed* with negative information is bad. Know your limits in listening to the news of the day or what others have to say, and honor these limits.
9. "Turn your face to the sun and the shadows fall behind you."—Maori proverb
10. One of the greatest things we can share with others is a sense of our own inner peace and a healthy perspective . . . but we can't share what we don't have. And so, healthy self-care is not just about us but also about the quality of our presence to others.
11. A true challenge in life today is seeing the times we feel vulnerable as portals to new wisdom before life returns to "normal."
12. "Disconnecting from change doesn't recapture the past, it loses the future."—Kathleen Norris
13. "You will never reach your destination if you stop and throw stones at every dog that barks."—Winston Churchill
14. Spending life waiting for the past to change results in missing the wonders of the present.
15. "In the second half of life, one of our major tasks is to withdraw our projections."—Carl Jung
16. Understanding our fears is a good way to prevent reacting with unnecessary anger and hate.

17. Who in your circle of friends represent the *prophet* who asks, "What voices from the past are guiding you in life?" Who also represents the *cheerleader*, who is supportive and sympathetic; the "*harasser*" or *teaser*, who prevents you from taking yourself too seriously; and the *inspirational friend*, who calls you to be all that you can be without embarrassing you that you are where you are at this point?
18. Discouragement is the last home of egoism in ourselves—look to the goodness around and beyond yourself for a healthier perspective when feeling down.
19. "The brighter the light, the deeper the darkness."—Carl Jung
20. Personal and professional faithfulness, *not* success, is a worthy goal.
21. When we psychologically prune our talents and gifts, they blossom and become richer. Remember to do this at each stage of life.
22. One of the most serious blocks to careful and fruitful *self*-mentoring is narcissism.
23. Quiet time alone is a gentle teacher when we approach ourselves with a spirit of intrigue.
24. The three blind alleys of self-reflection, mindfulness, and meditation are arrogance (where we project the blame on others), ignorance (where we condemn ourselves), and discouragement (because we wish change to take place when we want and in the form we want).
25. Being compassionate is pure heaven; toxic compassion though is pure hell. Know the difference and act in a way that has you extend yourself but not let yourself be psychologically drowned by the very person you are trying to rescue.
26. A fear of indebtedness is a very serious block to a spontaneous life of appreciating all the gifts around us and everything people are sharing with us.
27. *Self*-forgiveness makes space to learn what you may have done wrong in the past so you can live a more enlightened life in the present moment.
28. Fantasy uses up all the energy to make life better; dreaming uses up almost all the energy but saves enough for action to make future changes possible.
29. On the way to taking the important things in life seriously, it is very easy to take a mental detour and wind up taking *yourself* too seriously. Tease yourself more often. As Thomas Merton once reminded us, "The false self doesn't like to be laughed at."
30. Yogi Berra reminded us, in a way only he could, that "the future is not what it used to be." Being open helps us learn and make the most of life by dealing with the only constant: *change*.

And for those months that have 31 days, I would just end this month of reflection with some of the key elements of a resilient style, which usually include

- a psychological, spiritual, philosophical, or religious belief that centers you as someone who models such a sense of love, a healthy perspective, compassion, and resilience;
- an optimistic outlook that avoids the extremes of defeatism, on the one hand, and spiritual or psychological romanticism, on the other hand;
- an ability to hold current reality in the one hand and possibility going forward in the other hand to set the stage for action. For instance, during a lockdown, a person with this ability will find nurturing activities and encounters with others in their family that they may not have had time for in the past and might lament in the future;
- a recognition that resilience is a communal process so it is important to find and access a solid social support system; and
- a discerning eye as to recognizing what one can have an influence on and, as the saying goes, have the serenity to accept what can't be changed. This is essential because the self only has so much energy, so it is best to put it to work on what and where you can have an impact.

Works Cited

Corbett, R. (2016). *You must change your life.* New York, NY: Norton.

Dillard, A. (1989). *The writing life.* New York, NY: HarperCollins.

Ellsberg, R. (2003). *The saints' guide to happiness.* New York, NY: North Point Press.

France, P. (2002). *Patmos: A place of healing for the soul.* New York, NY: Atlantic Monthly Press.

Georiou, S. (2002). *Way of the dreamcatcher.* Ottawa, Ontario, Canada: Novalis.

Grumbach, D. (1994). *Fifty days of solitude.* Boston, MA: Beacon.

Hoff, B. (1992). *The Te of Piglet.* New York, NY: Dutton.

Klein, G. W. (1995). *All but my life: A memoir.* New York, NY: Hill & Wang.

Kornfield, J. (2000). *After the ecstasy, the laundry.* New York, NY: Bantam.

Lapsley, M. (2012). *Redeeming the past.* Maryknoll, NY: Orbis.

Maitland, S. (2003). *A book of silence.* Berkeley, CA: Counterpoint.

Norris, K. (1993). *Dakota.* Boston, MA: Houghton Mifflin.

Penny, L. (2019). *Kingdom of the blind.* New York, NY: St. Martin's.

Rilke, R. M. (1934). *Letters to a young poet.* New York, NY: Norton.

Suzuki, S. (2002). *Not always so* (E. Espe Brown, Ed.). New York, NY: HarperCollins.

Szasz, T. (1973). *The second sin.* New York, NY: Anchor.

White, T. H. (1958). *The once and future king.* New York, NY: Putnam.

Whyte, D. (2015). *Consolations.* Langley, WA: Many Rivers Press.

Wicks, R. J. (2003). *Riding the dragon: 10 lessons in inner strength in challenging times.* Notre Dame, IN: Sorin Books.

Wicks, R. J. (2010). *Bounce: Living the resilient life.* New York, NY: Oxford University Press.

Wicks, R. J. (2014). *Perspective: The calm within the storm.* New York, NY: Oxford University Press.

Wicks, R. J. (2018). *Night call: Embracing compassion and hope in a troubled world.* New York, NY: Oxford University Press.

About the Author

Robert J. Wicks, PsyD, is a world-recognized "resiliency psychologist" who was once referred to as "a master craftsman of hope" by best-selling inspirational writer Joyce Rupp. For more than 35 years, he has been called upon to speak calm into chaos by individuals and groups experiencing great stress, anxiety, and confusion.

He received his doctorate in psychology from Hahnemann Medical College and Hospital; is Professor Emeritus at Loyola University Maryland; and has taught in universities and professional schools of psychology, medicine, nursing, theology, education, and social work.

In 2003 he was the commencement speaker for Wright State School of Medicine in Dayton, Ohio, and in 2005 he was both visiting scholar and the commencement speaker at Stritch School of Medicine in Chicago. He was also the commencement speaker at and the recipient of honorary doctorates from Georgian Court University and Caldwell College in New Jersey and Marywood University in Pennsylvania.

In the past several years, he has spoken on his major areas of expertise—resilience, self-care, and the prevention of *secondary* stress (the pressures encountered in reaching out to others)—on Capitol Hill to members of Congress and their chiefs of staff and at Johns Hopkins School of Medicine, the U.S. Air Force Academy, the Mayo Clinic, the North American Aerospace Defense Command, the Defense Intelligence Agency, as well as Boston's Children's Hospital, Harvard Divinity School, Yale School of Nursing, Princeton Theological

Seminary, and the NATO Intelligence Fusion Center in England. He has also spoken at the Boston Public Library's commemoration of the Boston Marathon bombing; addressed 10,000 educators in the Air Canada Arena in Toronto; spoken at the FBI and New York City Police Academies; led a course on resilience in Beirut for relief workers from Aleppo, Syria; and addressed caregivers in China, Vietnam, India, Thailand, Haiti, Northern Ireland, Scotland, Hungary, Guatemala, Malta, New Zealand, Australia, France, England, and South Africa. In addition, he was the opening keynote speaker to 1,500 physicians for the American Medical Directors Association.

In 1994, he was responsible for the psychological debriefing of relief workers evacuated from Rwanda during the genocide. In 1993, and again in 2001, he worked in Cambodia with professionals from the English-speaking community who were present to help the Khmer people rebuild their nation following years of terror and torture. In 2006, he delivered presentations on self-care at both the National Naval Medical Center in and Walter Reed Army Hospital in Bethesda, Maryland, to health care professionals responsible for Iraq and Afghan war veterans evacuated to the United States with multiple amputations and severe head injuries. More recently, he addressed U.S. Army health care professionals returning from Africa, where they were assisting during the Ebola crisis.

In the military, he served as an officer in the U.S. Marine Corps. In that capacity, he was a field communications officer and also served as coordinator of treatment for military correctional facilities in Okinawa in the Ryukyu Islands of Japan and at Camp LeJeune in North Carolina.

He has published more than 50 books for both professionals and the general public, including the best-selling *Riding the Dragon* (Sorin Books, 2003/2012). Among his latest books from Oxford University Press for the general public are *Night Call: Embracing Compassion and Hope in a Troubled World* (2018); *Perspective: The Calm Within the Storm* (2014); and *Bounce: Living the Resilient Life* (2010). His books have been translated into Chinese, Korean, Indonesian, Polish, and Spanish. In 2006, he received the first annual Alumni Award for Excellence in Professional Psychology from Widener University. He is also the recipient of the Humanitarian of the Year Award from the American Counseling Association's Division on Spirituality, Ethics and Religious Values in Counseling.